The Teacher's Guide to National Board Certification

The Teacher's Guide to National Board Certification
Unpacking the Standards

Adrienne Mack-Kirschner

HEINEMANN
Portsmouth, NH

HEINEMANN
A division of Reed Elsevier Inc.
361 Hanover Street
Portsmouth, NH 03801–3912
www.heinemann.com

Offices and agents throughout the world

The author and the publisher wish to thank those who have generously given permission to reprint borrowed material:

Cover image of the National Board Certification box used courtesy of the National Board for Professional Teaching Standards.

Library of Congress Cataloging-in-Publication Data
Mack-Kirschner, Adrienne, 1944–

 The teacher's guide to National Board certification : unpacking the standards / Adrienne Mack-Kirschner.
  p. cm.
 Includes bibliographical references.
 ISBN 0-325-00549-4
 1. National Board for Professional Teaching Standards (U.S.)—Handbooks, manuals, etc. 2. Teachers—Certification—Standards—United States—Handbooks, manuals, etc. 3. Teaching—Standards—United States—Handbooks, manuals, etc. I. Title.

LB1771 .M27 2003
379.1′57—dc22   2002014464

Editor: Lois Bridges
Production service: Lisa S. Garboski, bookworks
Production coordination: Elizabeth Valway
Cover design: Lisa Fowler
Typesetter: Argosy Publishing
Manufacturing: Steve Bernier

Printed in the United States of America on acid-free paper
07 06 05 04 03 ML   2 3 4 5

This book is dedicated to my husband and best friend,
Stuart Barry Kirschner.

He remains my best teacher, the one who has taught me the most
about love.

Contents

Acknowledgments

I hardly know where or how to begin thanking all the people who have contributed to this book, directly and indirectly. Thanks go to my parents, Bill and Esther Daniels, who taught their three daughters that education can never be taken away from you and who, in spite of considerable financial hardships, made certain we were able to go to college. Certainly I want to thank my sister Royce Bellatty who was the first teacher in our family. My five children, Nadine McLane, Eric Mack, Christine Simon, Roxanne Ross, and Genevieve Mack, who collectively taught me how to talk to teenagers; they were my first students. It was their leaving home to pursue their own studies that created the gap in my life I would fill by becoming a high school teacher, a journey that eventually led to this book.

My professional mentors have been numerous, more than I could possibly acknowledge within these short pages. Joan Leibman was my first master teacher and remains a close personal friend. Linda Flammer allowed me to practice in her classroom and it is to her that I credit my ease in taking risks in teaching. Alisa Guthrie saved me with her advice when I was close to burning out: *Don't ever do anything a student can and should do.* Lisa Jones-Rath, my team teacher and great buddy, pushed all my buttons and wouldn't accept anything less from herself or me than great teaching. Eva Mayoral taught me to look at each student and value what each brought to the classroom.

I couldn't have written this book if it had not been for RaeJeane Williams and Jane Hancock and the California Writing Project. The Writing Project was the workshop where I learned I could write. It gave me voice and continues to influence how I think about teaching and how I learn by writing. RaeJeane listened to me talk for two years about wanting to become a National Board Certified Teacher (NBCT). She turned the dream into reality by providing the forum for the first NB support group. Together we brazenly confronted Sid Thompson, the superintendent of the state's largest school district and Day Higuchi, the president of the teachers' union, who together helped us to institutionalize support for teachers seeking Board certification in Los Angeles.

My knowledge about the National Board process has been deepened through the efforts of Judy Shulman, Joan Peterson, and Misty Sato at WestEd in San Francisco, and by my own journey to certification. I want to thank the National Board staff and Directors who continually strive to define accomplished teaching and to lay the foundation for quality teaching everywhere. Most especially I want to thank all the teacher candidates I am privileged to work with as they pursue Board certification and from whom I continue to learn about teaching.

Introduction

My life as a teacher began a few years after my fortieth birthday, following several successful careers as a mother, an entrepreneur, and a corporate executive. While each had elements that were very satisfying, especially my life as a mother, at midcareer I had a desire to do work that was important and meaningful, to make a positive difference in the world. And so I turned to education, to a reinvented self as a high school language arts teacher.

A year of required teacher credentialing classes, two wonderful master teachers while I completed a second year of student teaching, and I was ready. In spite of my advanced years (after all I wasn't an inexperienced twenty-something, but a seasoned veteran of the workplace), I was still woefully unprepared for the demands of the classroom. The university teacher preparation program hadn't adequately prepared me for thirty-plus teenagers every fifty-five minutes, no time for bathroom breaks or leisurely lunches, papers to grade, students' needs to consider and respond to, administrative regulations to adhere to, parents to consider, lessons to prepare. I would attest before any forum that teaching is the most difficult, albeit the most rewarding and most important, job in the world. My dilemma was how to do it well without getting burned out.

It was only after I had a classroom of my own, without the daily guidance of a supervising teacher, that I understood the teacher preparation I had received prepared me to teach at a novice level. Developing the art and craft of a master teacher is a lifelong process, and I was determined to become a master craftsperson.

For six years I attended every workshop our district offered. I went on field trips to visit authentic sites of the Chumash Indians. I spent Saturdays at the music center studying opera as literature, and evenings in the art museum developing multiple ways of seeing, converting the concrete to the abstract and back again. Somewhere out there, I was convinced, were the secrets for becoming an accomplished teacher. I searched everywhere, followed every education guru who promised the answers, read the latest research to discover how to reach all students. The guru, I determined, would have to come from within me, homegrown and nurtured by all I could glean from those who went before me.

That's when I discovered the National Board for Professional Teaching Standards (NBPTS)—a prototype for what accomplished practice looks like. Models for entry-level teacher benchmarks abound; what I found in the NBPTS was a model for accomplished teaching that I could emulate, guiding questions that would help me to reflect upon my own practice. The questions were the key: What are your goals for your students? Why are these goals important? How will you know when a student reaches them? What will you do to continue students' growth? How do you continue to learn and develop as an educator? In the Jewish tradition children are not asked what they did in school each day, the parent wants to know if they asked any good questions. That's what the National Board does, it asks you questions about your practice, and it's in thinking through how to answer that you further develop your proficiency as an educator.

I decided that I wanted to challenge the National Board process and attain certification. I knew, however, that I would have a much higher chance of attaining certification, and would learn a great deal more, if I could work through the process with other teachers rather than attempt to tackle the daunting portfolio requirements on my own. Before there were any support programs or National Board Certified Teachers to guide us; before financial incentives or local recognition were in place, eighteen of us undertook this professional journey, opening our private teaching for public inspection. We began in a classroom, courageously determined to stick together until our portfolios were completed and our assessment center exercises on their electronic way. We began at the beginning, by unpacking the "box" the National Board used to send all the portfolio instructions, the standards, the forms, and mailing labels and envelopes to candidates. Included were explicit instructions not to dispose of the box as we'd be returning our completed portfolio entries and accompanying forms in the same FedEx box. We were all very much in awe of the "box."

When we met together to examine our students' work and use it as a guide for studying our teaching, we made genuine progress toward reaching all our students. Our tools were math and science and language arts, second-grade curriculum and fifth-, yet we were connected through our common goal of seeking how best to positively impact our students' lives in meaningful and important ways. The National Board process, analyzing and reflecting upon what students are learning and how our teaching adds value to them, has been the *yellow brick road* we followed. The journey, the lifelong learning, is the destination. Although the National Board awarded our certificates, it didn't make us accomplished teachers, it only publicly acknowledged that we are.

It's my journey, and the journey of the more than seven hundred teachers I have assisted during the past six years as they worked towards achieving certification, that informs this book. You may begin with any of the sections that follow, read from cover to cover, or jump around as inspiration moves you. In addition to the nuts and bolts of the *how to complete the portfolio*, you'll discover the premises behind everything the National Board process requires of you. You will find, as we did, that the resources to move each student to high levels of achievement are already within your reach. Instead of searching for that perfect strategy, that set of books which will help all children to learn, the guru—domestic or imported—who can lead the school or district in the reform of the moment, look to yourself and your students, call upon your colleagues and your community. Your ultimate professional goal may be achieving National Board Certification, but it is truly the journey, the National Board process, that makes this the most worthwhile professional development you will ever undertake. You will learn, as we have, that the journey, creating a professional portfolio, is the destination.

I salute and celebrate you, my fellow teachers. Yours is the most important job in the world.

The History

We need to study the history of public education to learn from what we have done in the past if we are to understand what we need to do to assure our students have the opportunity to be successful in this information-rich and demanding era. If we fail to critically examine the history and current status of public education, we may lose it to vouchers, private schools for the wealthy, and minimal standards for the rest of our students. The failure of our public education system to educate all children at high levels might signal the end of democracy as we know it. You may think I'm being melodramatic, but public education is at a crossroads. We, the practitioners, will either take charge of it or sit by and watch it devolve, creating an ever-widening chasm between those who have and those who have not. I feel passionately that teachers, working one classroom at a time, can make the difference. We are the largest profession in the country, the keepers of the nation. Traditionally, however, we have had little say in the evolution of education; the founders planned it just that way.

Public schools were intended to be governed by mostly male local school boards supervising mostly female low-status teachers. Teachers were kept in isolation, in buildings designed as individual cells, separated by grade and subject, much like an *egg crate* (See Tyack, 1974). As the number of students increased, schools became even more centrally controlled. The divide widened between those determining policy and those delivering the instruction. Classrooms developed idiosyncratically; the quality of education any student received was, and still is, dependent upon the teacher's content knowledge and ability to deliver that content to students. That many teachers consider the classroom their private domain remains a barrier to quality education for all students. Past efforts to "fix" broken schools have been centered on making central office changes, on restructuring the structure without touching the heart of teaching and learning, the individual classroom. What students were expected to learn, and how teachers would direct their instruction, remained in the hands of individual practitioners. Not only have students marched along without a clearly defined goal of what they are expected to know and be able to do, so have teachers.

The mid 1980s brought an interest across the nation in student performance standards—what students should know and be able to do at various benchmarks in their education. Immediately upon the introduction of common standards for all students followed the protest that *one size doesn't fit all*, that not every student can achieve high standards, or that the standards themselves are flawed—and some of them are. The list of those who should be excused from the requirement to demonstrate proficiency in a common set of performance standards, critics attest, include children of poverty, ethnic minorities, English language learners, and students with disabilities. Although I sincerely respect the good intentions and honest concerns of those who would not hold all students accountable for their learning, I am adamant that clearly delineated performance standards, with multiple opportunities for students to reach them, is the only way to preserve our democracy and to prepare our children to enter a competitive global economy and to have choices in their lives. For a more thorough discussion of using standards to promote learning than is possible in these pages, consult Beverly Falk's *The Heart of the Matter*. It is our job, as educators, to teach with the same high expectations for all students. To do so, we must first assure that teachers are capable of, and required to, teach to those high standards. The National Board for Professional Teaching Standards is a natural, and rightful, adjunct to student performance standards. (Okay, I know my passion is showing. I'll get off the soapbox now, but will undoubtedly mount it again.)

In 1986, the Carnegie task force offered a solution to the nationally perceived, if exaggerated, woes of education:

> The key to success lies in creating a profession equal to the task—a profession of well-educated teachers prepared to assume new powers and responsibilities to redesign schools for the future.

Even if their reason for being was poorly founded, their findings continue to be supported. The quality of the teacher is the single most important factor in the education of a child. It was logical that the task force urge the teaching profession to set standards and certify teachers who meet those standards. It called for the formation of the National Board for Professional Teaching Standards (NBPTS). The National Board remains a nonprofit, nonpartisan, and nongovernmental agency with classroom teachers holding a majority of the seats on the sixty-three-member board of directors.

The Board's mission is clearly focused on improving the quality of teaching and learning by:

- "Maintaining high and rigorous standards for what accomplished teachers should know and be able to do,

- "Providing a national voluntary system certifying teachers who meet these standards, and
- "Advocating related education reforms to integrate National Board Certification in American education and to capitalize on the expertise of National Board Certified Teachers."

(For a complete history of the National Board, consult the website: *www.nbpts.org/about_us* .)

The National Board reflects the research data that points to the quality of the teacher as the most important factor impacting student learning. Unlike all the recent school reforms that focus on school structure, curriculum, shared decision making, block scheduling, houses, and more, the National Board focus is on teachers and students. Focusing on the quality of instruction and student learning, the NBPTS can be the most significant reform to improve our schools and provide an environment where every student can learn at high levels.

Even though all states currently have some standards in place, there remains controversy about student performance standards, which are not different in purpose from the standards for teachers. Several years ago, when the *language arts standards* came to my school district, I introduced them to my high school journalism students. At first they were shocked that they were going to be held to a set of standards in order to graduate. Accruing 220 credits had been the criteria for graduation, and some students were savvy enough to know you could accumulate credits with Ds as easily as you could with As. If my class of mostly seniors was unaware of the student performance standards, we reasoned, then there was a good chance the rest of the student body was also ignorant. Since I was the journalism advisor the class thought it would be a good idea to co-author an essay we could publish in the school paper. In class we debated whether or not students should be accountable for achieving the standards. Here's what senior Antonio R. wrote on September 26, 1998:

> All products in the US have to meet certain standards. Students are the products of the US education system. Therefore, all students should have to meet these high standards or not graduate until they do. A high school diploma is not good enough unless it's proof of students' accomplishments.

I couldn't have said it better. Hugh G. added that meeting the standards "will make a student better prepared for the future." To not meet the standards, "graduates," according to Bertha P., "will be worried about being laid off and being replaced by a smarter person." Michal G. believes "they [the standards] are not only the standards for a classroom they are the standards for a successful life."

If we hold students accountable to a set of performance standards, why not teachers? After all, Andrea O. argued, "The basic standards can easily be met as long as teachers are willing to teach through the school years; students become aware of what is expected of them and therefore are encouraged to meet their goals."

At a time in education when many states face massive teacher shortages, and where nearly anyone with a college degree can be hired as a teacher, we are more in need of teaching performance standards than ever before. Standing in front of a group of students and recording grades in a roll book is simply not acceptable. While teachers don't need scripted programs, they do need guidelines. We need to know what high-quality teaching looks like so we can grow into accomplished teachers. The National Board standards present this blueprint for accomplished teaching.

All the work of the National Board is based upon five core propositions:

1. Teachers are committed to students and their learning.

2. Teachers know the subjects they teach and how to teach those subjects to students.

3. Teachers are responsible for managing and monitoring student learning.

4. Teachers think systematically about their practice and learn from experience.

5. Teachers are members of learning communities.

In the next chapters we'll examine each of the core propositions, what they say, what they mean, and why they matter so much. We'll apply them to the guiding questions in the portfolio instructions and consider the nature of the evidence one might find in an exemplary classroom practice that supports the standards. Along the way we'll continually take your pulse by doing a personal inventory to self-evaluate where you are as a practitioner and how you can continue to develop the wizard within.

Consult the National Board website for the complete text of the Core Propositions: *www.nbpts.org/core_propositions.*

Core Proposition 1

Teachers Are Committed to Students and Their Learning

1

The five core propositions are the basis for all the National Board Standards. While all the propositions are critically important, none is more essential than a sincere belief that all students can learn. It is appropriate that the National Board lists this proposition first.

In my work with teachers over the past eight years, I have too often encountered those who vocalize a belief in their students' abilities, but whose classroom practice belies it. Since we teach our students based upon what we believe about them, if we don't believe they can learn at high levels, for whatever reasons—poverty, ethnicity, social status, primary language, or education level of their parents—then we won't teach them at high levels. Our practice will exhibit *domesticating education* activities, not *liberating and empowering* ones (Finn, 1999). When they don't achieve we'll blame it on outside factors over which we have no control, rather than on our own teaching. But no matter what excuses we might offer, student achievement is dependent primarily upon us. The quality of the teaching is the single most important factor in a child's education. As the classroom teacher, it is our responsibility to become the absolutely best teacher we can be. Our charge is to teach to high, rigorous standards, providing multiple opportunities so all students can learn.

To test your own beliefs about student learning, try this simple reflection: Say—Mean—Matter

Instructions:

1. What do you say about your students? List ten words or phrases that come to mind when you think or talk to others about your students.

2. What does what you say, mean? Read your list. What do these words and phrases imply about what you believe about your students?

3. Why does what you say and mean about your students' learning matter so much? How does your belief about your students affect your teaching? The work you assign? Your expectations for them? Your expectations for yourself as a teacher?

Sometimes we hold beliefs about our students which we've never thought about. Howard Gardner indicates that these deeply held, unquestioned beliefs, remain with us as a result of the *unschooled mind*. Often, our beliefs are fixed by the time we are about five years old. Without examination notions that may have formed early, remain. These misconceptions, however, can be changed by examining them, finding their root causes, testing them against what we see around us, and being vigilant they don't recur. If you discover through this reflection that you do hold low expectations for some or all of your students, find that student, or those students, whose work surpassed your expectations. Examine those students' work samples. Analyzing enough of those examples might dispel the beliefs you've held for certain groups of students. It's only when we believe all our students can learn, that we strive to make powerful knowledge accessible to all of them.

A commitment to students and their learning has many layers. What follows is an analysis of some of the key ideas imbedded in this core proposition.

Key Point: Recognizing Individual Differences

Accomplished teachers not only recognize that students have individual differences, they seek out those differences, build on them, and find ways to use those differences to make content meaningful. Students are different in how they learn, and in what they learn. Accomplished teachers can apply the theories of Multiple Intelligences (Gardner, 1999) as well as Goldman's work on *Emotional Intelligence* (1997). We have to know our students well beyond their past scholastic achievements and the test scores recorded on cumulative student records. We also have to know about them as individuals, knowledge gained through talking to them and providing multiple opportunities for them to share what they do in their free time, who they spend time with, and where they go when they are not in school. We can learn about out students' individuality by listening to them and by watching them interact with their peers. An excellent method for learning more about our students is an exercise I do with my National Board candidates.

The Community Walk

The Community Walk is similar in nature to a school *walk-through* whereby a school leader takes time to walk through a classroom or group of classrooms in order to absorb the "flavor" of the teaching and learning on any given day. The school walk-through is a precursor to deeper observations, not a replacement for them. The Community Walk has a similar purpose—to learn about the social context and experiences of the students attending the school.

Many educators don't live near the schools where they teach. They experience the school neighborhood only while driving through on the way to school or home from work. We see our students differently, and more fully, when we take the time to walk their walk and to see their sights. Just as we learn more about our colleagues' teaching when we actually observe them in their classrooms, we can learn more about our students by seeing their communities. Just like school Learning Walks capture a sense of what is happening at school, a community learning walk can capture the context of our students' lives.

The challenge of getting to know our students, their interests, backgrounds, and prior knowledge, requires us to use many tools including surveys, letters from and to their homes, autobiographical writings, sharing of hobbies and other outside school interests. Familiarity with the communities where our students live is another powerful way to know our students.

Instructions for the Community Walk

Take a walk through the neighborhood where your school is located. Plan an hour, if you can. Walk with a colleague, if that is more comfortable, but agree not to talk too much to one another. Concentrate on absorbing the sights and sounds of the neighborhood. If you think you already know the neighborhood well (perhaps you live there), take your walk down streets you don't usually follow. Visit some stores you've never entered before. In preparation, you might ask your students about some sights worth seeing, stores worth visiting, community characters to watch for. Create a loose plan in advance for what you'll want to do. Perhaps you'll visit a religious center, a student's home, the local market. Stay flexible. Plans can be made, and just as readily changed. Don't ignore the unexpected teachable moments that might arise. Bring a camera along and then make a scrapbook your students can add to. Be open and ready to learn. Be prepared to be surprised.

A wonderful variation on the self-directed Community Walk is to ask your students to bring to class pictures of their neighborhood. One first-grade teacher of English language learners, working toward National Board Certification, wrote a grant that enabled her to buy disposable cameras for each of her students. The youngsters took photos and then used them to write stories about their lives. The resulting annotated photos not only informed the teacher about her students, but gave her insight to some of the factors influencing their learning, and thus her teaching. She empowered her students, building upon what they knew, to move them into reading and writing, even though many of them came from homes where the literacy level was low. The original funders invited her to take her classroom photos on tour, which she did.

Learning happens in a social context. The more we know about our students' social context, the more ways we have to reach them. Seeing where and how our students live, especially if their lives are very different from our own, helps us to understand their intelligence, which may not always be demonstrated on the norm-referenced tests popular today. When we learn more about our students' lives, we have additional ways of helping them connect what they already know to the new learning we are offering.

Reflection on the Community Walk

Because we learn, not through our experiences alone, but by processing those experiences, the Community Walk would not be complete without taking time for reflection. If you don't already have one, now is a good time for you to begin maintaining a teaching journal. In the journal you can jot down your thoughts at the end of the day, record any teachable moments (the ones you feel sure you'll remember, but invariably forget), reexamine what happened during a lesson, with a student, as a result of something you read. For this reflection, we'll use the same writing genres the National Board portfolio entries require—Description, Analysis, and Reflection.

- Description (another way of saying What?): Describe what you did. How long you walked. Where you went. Who or what you saw or heard.
- Analysis (So what?): What did you expect to see, hear, and learn? What did you learn? What surprised you? What beliefs about the neighborhood were confirmed? What beliefs were challenged? Cite specific examples from your walk as evidence.
- Reflection (Then what?): What understandings will return to the classroom with you? How will these new understandings impact your teaching? Your students' learning?

In addition to learning more about your students, an added bonus of the Community Walk is making connections with the community. One of the National Board entries, Entry 4—documented accomplishments, asks you to document what you do to reach out to the community and families of your students. Walking through the neighborhood is a beginning. You might find a business you can partner with; learn about the existence of a local Rotary or Lions Club; find a group of parents anxious to participate at the school. Communities are rich resources we often disregard in our frenzy to teach the required curriculum and prepare our students for the tests mandated each year.

The Teacher's Guide to National Board Certification

Key Point: Child Development and Learning Theory

Another key factor of this first core proposition requires that teachers have a knowledge of child development and how students learn. While the National Board does not expect teachers to be scholars in the area of child development, a working knowledge of the developmental stages is critical.

Teachers should be familiar with social learning theory, a theory espoused by Albert Bandura and others, that identifies that learning happens as a result of modeling, retention, physical reproduction, and motivation. You don't need to recall the researchers responsible for any particular theory. No need to quote names or cite sources. It is sufficient to understand how theory relates to classroom practice. For example, accomplished teachers *model* the skills we want students to acquire. We can influence learning *retention* rates by providing multiple opportunities to learn and relearn the targeted skills. Writing about a new learning aids retention, as does *physically reproducing* it. Student *motivation* is highest when they understand why they are being asked to do a particular task, and how that task relates to tasks they've undertaken in the past, and will relate to challenges in the future.

When we understand how learning happens we can select teaching strategies to magnify positive results. Even though child developmental stages are not exact and there's a wide range among students, when we know the basics we can provide experiences for our students that are developmentally appropriate.

Here's how I put theory into practice. My teaching changed dramatically when I read, in a brief article, and discussed with colleagues, an explanation of Lev Vygotsky's Zone of Proximal Development. In short, Vygotsky confirmed that we learn based on what we already know, plus a little more. Teach way above the students' current knowledge, and they're lost. Teach below their ability, and they're bored and unmotivated. Teach to what they know plus a bit more, and they make the leap. In the classroom, that translates into scaffolding, a method by which we move students toward higher learning incrementally; the goal is independence, the scaffold provides support during the learning. I learned to slow down and catch the students where they were, then to move them along, sometimes pulling, other times pushing. I could have continued teaching at a level where they should have been, according to the state frameworks, even though they were several grades below that level. Instead, I went back to catch them where they knew the work. We then moved along, quite rapidly, to where they needed to be. I felt more successful and they were a lot less frustrated. Reading about the zone of proximal development is one example of how I moved theory into action.

So, how do very busy teachers assure their practice is grounded in the best and most current education theories? Not an easy task given the demands to keep up with subject matter, reach out to parents and the community, serve on an abundant number of committees, and still have time for an occasional movie. There is hope and help out there. It is now easier to find sources that are authoritative and relevant to our classroom practices, and that are also accessible, not written in edu-jargon decipherable only by the university researcher. I use Google, a search engine rich in education resources, driven by key words common to my teaching practice. I talk to my colleagues, read a couple of teaching journals, pick up user-friendly books at conferences. Most of all, I pay attention to the feedback I get from my students, by closely examining the work they do and listening to what they tell me. I read and grade student work to learn what they know and how I might build on their knowledge.

Key Point: Accomplished Teachers Treat Their Students Equally— Not to Be Confused With Treating Them All the Same.

I remember many years ago, long before I even considered teaching as a career move, a group of teachers reporting on a study they had read. They said that students who came to school better dressed than their peers, clean and neat, received more attention from the teacher. Although this could be one of those urban legends because I've never been able to find the original source for their comments, it's worth considering. If this statement has merit, it means that the better-dressed elementary student, who would receive more of the teacher's attention, would progress more rapidly. An early start lays the foundation for future educational success. And because we learn based on what we already know, the more students know, the more they will learn. Imagine—the fate of many of our students may be at least partially determined by how well dressed they are when they enter the classroom. I look at elementary pictures of myself and see way too large hand-me-down dresses, socks lacking elastic, and scuffed shoes. I wonder what the teachers thought. We each need to examine our personal biases and make certain that they do not interfere with all of our students receiving equitable treatment.

The National Board expends a great deal of time and money training assessors to score your portfolio entries and assessment center exams. Much of the training is focused on uncovering and then removing any biases that may impact the scores, either favorably or unfavorably. As accomplished teachers, we should do the same. Does the student with the loud voice set your teeth on edge? What about the ones who tug at your sleeve, "Teacher, teacher, teacher" until you wish they'd go away? My friend Steve Garelick paraphrases Will Rogers' famous line about not having met a person he didn't like. Steve says that he's never met a person he couldn't like. It's a good attitude to take into the classroom as well. Find something lovable about every child who walks into your room. It's there. Sometimes we just have to dig a little deeper to find those special differences. *Reflection:* Think about a student you find "unattractive" or "difficult." Now think about something wonderful that student brings to class. Don't quit until you do.

Key Point: Students With Exceptional Needs

The trend in education is to mainstream children to the least restrictive environment. That means that we are more and more likely to have children in our classrooms with special needs—learning disabilities, mild retardation, and physical handicaps. It's tempting to identify a child as the "kid in the wheelchair," or as "the Ritalin kid." But no child can be completely represented by one characteristic. We need to be vigilant in seeing the whole child, and in teaching to the whole child. I am especially sensitive to teachers' comments discounting students with special needs because my granddaughter is one of those students. She has cerebral palsy and walks with the assistance of two canes. She sometimes needs a wheelchair to get around on the playground. But when she smiles, she's missing the same two front teeth as her first-grade peers. She laughs at *Shrek* and squeals riding the roller coaster in our local amusement park. I urge her teachers to see her in light of what she can do, which is almost everything any other seven-year-old can do, and not by what she can't do, which is walk without assistance.

Find something lovable in each child who enters your classroom. Work a little harder to love even those you initially find annoying. The more love we give away, the more that's returned.

Another Key Point to Think About: We Teach Children First, Then the Curriculum.

My primary teaching experience is at the secondary level, grades 8 through 12, where many of my colleagues are prone to teach the content of their subjects, forgetting that our mission is first to teach children. How do we tap into what students already know, assist them in making connections between seemingly disparate ideas, bridge multiple disciplines in order to aid students as they attempt to make sense of the world around them? What are those essential big ideas in each discipline that we need to know in order to understand the content? How to teach those big ideas without getting lost in too many details? How do we balance students' emotional needs, honor their differences, and still teach them to successfully negotiate a very complex global society? Accomplished teachers strive to do all the above. They come to the classroom armed with theory and experience; they learn by doing and redoing; they listen to their students' voices and critically examine student outcomes. Our job as professional educators is far more complex than any I held in the business community. Nevertheless, we can take a lesson from the marketplace. Consider the client first. Our clients are our students. Accomplished teaching is not about what the teacher does; we don't work in a vacuum. It's about student learning and helping all students to achieve at the highest levels they are able to reach.

The National Board Portfolio—Knowing Our Students

Teachers' knowledge of their students, and the context of their teaching environment, is called on throughout the portfolio entries. Teachers are expected to know the larger context of their teaching environment—their district and school data—and the features of their class(es) that impact their approach to teaching. The National Board portfolio instructions for each entry include guiding questions that call upon teachers' knowledge of their students.

At the school level, you're asked about grade levels and the number of students in the class featured in the entry, as well as the subject matter being taught. At the classroom level, the entry requires more detail. What are those *relevant* characteristics that influence your instruction in the class featured in the entry? What about the ethnicity, cultural backgrounds, linguistic diversity, and range of abilities of your students? Any personality features you need to note? What do we need to know about the students with exceptional needs?

The key word in the guiding questions is *relevant*. The characteristics you record should be those you consider when you plan your instruction.

A social studies/history candidate I worked with during the 2001–2002 cycle did an excellent job enumerating the features of his class. He described the limited language proficiency of his students, their cultural background as first-generation immigrants from several Central American countries, and their wide range of demonstrated abilities and interests he'd discovered through a survey he had each student complete. He'd spent considerable time and energy in gathering this data. But when in the very next paragraph of his portfolio entry he went on to list his instructional goals, the goals had no connection to his students. The lessons were ones he'd been teaching for years. He made no effort to bridge the cultural gap between what his students already knew and where he wanted to lead them. The lesson bombed, the students were lost, and he didn't understand why until he sat with his colleagues, myself among them, and talked about what happened.

While the immediate purpose for describing your district, school, and class context is to allow the assessor who will be scoring your entry to "see" the class and to understand it, the long-term, and more important, goal of thinking about your students is so you will be able to provide the most relevant instruction for them, at this time in their education.

Another guiding question in the portfolio directions asks about the instructional challenges your class presents. Those challenges may include, but would not be limited to, discipline and motivation, cognitive levels, and the time of day the class meets—after lunch can be an extra challenge. Challenges aren't necessarily only found with low-performing students. Shelia, an EA/ELA candidate, taught identified gifted students. Her challenge was to continually provide enough intellectual stimulation for a very highly motivated, grade-conscious, group of students. If it didn't immediately relate to boosting SAT scores, they didn't want any of what she had to offer. Challenges can be with high- and low-achieving students. Every class has its own collective personality, and each presents a challenge. Accomplished teachers consider each class to have individual needs and adjust the lessons accordingly. While ideally it would be great as a secondary teacher to develop one lesson plan for all five of your ninth-grade classes, it probably won't work out that way. Something about "the best-laid plans"! Accomplished teachers adjust their lessons to their classes' needs.

In addition to knowing the greater context of your district and school, as well as the particular attributes of the featured class, the portfolio requires that you know individual students as well.

The entries that focus on student work (entries 1–3 for most certificates) ask for specific information about the student(s) whose work is featured in the entry. Specifically, who is the student? You should understand and be prepared to articulate why you chose that student or those students. Weave information within the entry about the challenges this student presents, the particular goals you may have had for this student(s), and any unique characteristics you addressed as a teacher. *Caution:* don't list defining characteristics of the student(s) if you don't address them in your analysis. To say a student learns best through visual representation and then not to include a strategy that addresses this preference, is worse than not knowing the student. Providing differentiated instruction for each student is not an easy task. The core proposition reminds us that while we teach to a group, we teach individual children.

There's no doubt that a secondary teacher with five classes a day has a greater challenge in knowing 180 students than does an elementary teacher with 20. There are ways to know your students—surveys, letters from them to you, autobiographical incidents they write about, connections they make personally to the subject matter. Concentrate, during the year of your NB candidacy, on the class or classes you plan to feature. Your heightened awareness will still spread to all your other students. There is something very rewarding about seeing your students as individuals and caring about them. Knowing your students as individuals takes time. Candidates for certification do report spending more time with their students: hanging around during lunch, arriving earlier at school, staying later instead of hurrying off campus when the dismissal bell rings—and listening to what they have to say. The more I see my students as individuals, the more I enjoy my teaching.

Although the last class of teenagers I taught was in February 2001, I'm still a teacher with all the challenges of a pre-K–12 teacher, only my students are older, adult learners. I apply all I learned through studying the National Board core propositions to my current classrooms. I recently asked a group of precandidates to pull out what they considered the key points of core proposition 1. Here's what they identified as key elements:

Accomplished teachers

- Adjust and alter their lessons to best fit their students' needs
- Recognize individual differences and get to know their students, learn to read them, and acquire a deep understanding of them
- Understand how students develop and learn
- Know teaching theories
- Provide multiple contexts
- Remember that intelligence is culturally defined
- Treat students equitably remembering that similar treatment does not necessarily equal equitable education

Finally, accomplished teaching extends beyond cognitive capacity. Teachers help students to develop self-concept; they motivate, address student character, and instill civic virtues.

In summary—accomplished teachers teach the *whole* student.

It is important as you read through this book on unpacking the National Board Standards that you don't remain a bystander, and that you do become involved. Don't take my word that the key points I selected from any of the core propositions are the definitive learning to be gained. Teacher precandidates in my classes made selections that were both similar to and different from my own. Take the time to study the propositions and highlight those factors you consider key to accomplished teaching practice. The National Board process is not scripted or formulaic. There is opportunity for every teacher to provide evidence of best practices, and although best practices have much in common, they will also be individual. Trust yourself and your own understanding. Talk to colleagues and seek consensus around the key factors. Use this book as a guide, not as a final authority.

Core Proposition 2

Teachers Know the Subjects They Teach and How to Teach Those Subjects to Students

We come to the teaching profession through multiple paths and for varied reasons. Secondary teachers frequently begin with a deep love for and commitment to a particular discipline. One need only see the thousands of books on my library shelves to know love of reading and literature propelled me to the English Language Arts classroom. Others come more from a desire to be with young children than from a devotion to a specific subject. With the necessity to fill the expected hundreds of thousands of teacher vacancies over the next ten years, many states are seeking those in other fields who can bring their subject knowledge to the classroom—such as scientists and mathematicians. However we came to the classroom, however well we know our subject or subjects, content knowledge is only part of being an effective teacher. Knowing one's subject and how to teach that subject so youngsters can learn are the keys to this core proposition.

Secondary and itinerant teachers face increased challenges presented by the sheer number of students they work with daily. Elementary teachers, although they see fewer children each day, have the challenge of teaching multiple subjects. They are expected to know a dozen or more content areas while attending to the needs of their developing students. While the National Board does not expect a fourth-grade teacher to have the same command of biology as does a high school biology teacher, the elementary generalist, as well as the secondary specialist, is expected to know the big ideas in each discipline and how the disciplines relate to one another. Knowing the interconnectedness across subjects has increasing importance in an ever-shrinking world.

Futurist Peter Schwartz predicts that within the next dozen years, surely by 2020, available information will double every seventy-seven days. Because there is no way we can teach everything there is to know, helping students to identify key ideas and to extract major concepts has increased importance. The more content knowledge we possess, the better we understand the constructs of the discipline, the better we are able to assist students in organizing information and chunking it for future retrieval. We need to guide students to an understanding of the relationship between what they already know and what they are learning. Teachers must be comfortable within the disciplines they teach in order to be able to identify the concepts the children are grappling with as well as to correct any misconceptions they may have. Teachers' math phobia, for example, gets passed along to their students, often in quite unconscious comments. And so does their passion.

My cousin's twenty-year-old son recently completed his first year in college. It was an unnoteworthy year. Then he took a summer school class at a local community college and felt inspired. The subject, Black Studies, held no particular prior interest for him, so I inquired into why and how this class was special. After some discussion he said that the teacher loved her subject. She was passionate about it and brought lots of materials to supplement the textbook. Her passion inspired him in ways his other teachers had not. What are your passions? How can you bring them into the classroom?

How well do you know your subject(s)? In the candidate support groups I direct, working with pre-K–12 candidates across the content areas, we begin with the course outlines, the frameworks or content standards, for our grades and subjects. (For the purposes of this discussion, I will be referencing the California frameworks, because that's where I teach; you should substitute whatever state/district document directs your grade and/or subject.) The next few pages will take you through the steps to complete a personal inventory of your content knowledge. Remember, this core proposition is about content knowledge and ways to teach so students can learn.

Instructions

- Read (or skim) the introduction to the frameworks applicable to your teaching assignment. [I like to use Active Reading Symbols (see the Active Reading Symbols chart on page 19.)]
- The active reading symbols keep my mind more alert and help me to interact with the text as I read. I use the same model with my students.
- Using sticky notes, identify the sections of the frameworks you are required to teach—usually grade-level sections.
- Read and mark the sections preceding and following your assignment. This is what the youngsters coming to you should know, but may not. More important, what follows your grade curriculum is what they should know and be able to do when they leave your class.
- Return to the section(s) that pertain to your current teaching assignment, determine the major themes, concepts, or "big ideas" that emerge across the standards (see Major Themes chart on page 19).
- List each of the major themes down the left-hand side. (You will most likely need several tables to cover all the major themes. Elementary and middle school generalists will need at least one for each discipline they teach.)

Active Reading Symbols	
A	I agree
X	I disagree or I need help
+	New information
?	I need clarification or I wonder about that
???	Don't get it
!!!	WOW
÷	I can do this

- Fill in column 2. (You may want to differentiate between what you know and teach well versus what you only touch upon.) Do you address multiple standards/disciplines in a single lesson/unit? If not, how might you become more interdisciplinary in your practice?
- Column 3 is critically important. You will want to know your content well prior to beginning the National Board candidacy year.
- What steps will you take to fill in the gaps in your content knowledge? (Excellent sources are professional organizations, subject matter projects, university courses designed for teachers, readings in the targeted discipline, articles, discussion groups. Don't omit the Internet as a powerful source of references and content. Consult your state department of education for professional development opportunities.)

Major Themes			
Major Themes	**What I currently know/teach**	**What I need to learn/teach**	**How I will fill in the gaps**

Key point: Accomplished Teachers Appreciate How Knowledge in Their Subjects is Created, Organized, and Linked to Other Disciplines.

Accomplished teachers know and are able to teach the facts, the discreet bits of information, but they also have a much bigger picture of how these factoids relate to one another and to information outside the specific subject. We are able to teach the interrelatedness of the world around us. We know that the cultural and economic dimensions of the rain forest, for example, extend beyond its pharmaceutical and biological importance. Literature evolves in an historical context and is enriched when studied from that lens. Historical events have a different impact depending on whose point of view we are studying. Even studying trees takes on a whole different meaning if we instruct students to wear the hats of the lumberjack, the environmentalist, or the botanist. The goal is to guide youngsters in thinking analytically about content and its relevance to the rest of the natural world.

Key Point: Accomplished Teachers Know How to Convey a Subject to Students.

I'm reminded of a cartoon I saw featuring a new teacher standing before the principal. The principal handed him the curriculum guide and a "bag of tricks," then wished him good luck. The strategies we use to convey information to students is much more complex than a bag of tricks. Each strategy, whether it's direct instruction or inquiry, whole or small group, should be appropriate to the context and the content. We have to know what the students already know, what misconceptions they might be carrying forward, and what related knowledge they have. Determining how to balance time spent on the content with time spent teaching a strategy as a way to acquire the content knowledge is no simple task. There is no single resource, like a textbook, that always does the trick. Teachers need to consider print texts, videotape, computer software, musical recordings, primary documents, the Internet, and more. The challenge is connecting the students, within their educational environment, to the content. The accomplished teacher continually makes conscious choices.

The Teacher's Guide to National Board Certification

Key Point: Teachers Generate Multiple Paths to Knowledge

There are occasions when structured, or directed, lessons are the best way to deliver information. There are other occasions, however, when helping students discover relationships, and uncover concepts, is the most effective approach. Making the finest choice comes from knowing the content, understanding the developmental readiness of the students, and having a deep "bag of tricks" from which to pull.

Accomplished teachers call on a wide range of sources, print and non-print, textbook and primary sources, interviews and case studies. They teach about the reliability of each different source, that dot-coms have products to sell and that while dot-edus usually don't sell conventional products, they are about selling themselves and their ideas. Accomplished teachers assign individual tasks and group projects with the knowledge and experience that instructional goals are best met in a variety of ways. They respect students' learning styles and help them to stretch from what comes most easily to what requires taking an educational leap.

Accomplished teachers help students to pose questions, some of which may not have an immediate answer or any answer at all. Asking, then grappling with answering, questions they themselves pose moves students into higher-order thinking.

I like to use a technique, a variation of one many educators use, with my students that helps the class to generate the areas they wish to study. The technique is frequently referred to as KWL: what students *know*, what they *want* to know, and what they *learned*. My variation differentiates what they *know* from what they *think* they know.

KWL

I usually begin KWL with a word or a concept. (We can use the word *crocodile*, for example.) Students first list individually all they know about crocodiles. I ask them to separate those things they know for sure—the facts they would risk their allowance on—from what they think might be true, but are unsure of. Once each student has a list, they work in groups combining to move the "not sures" to the "sure" column and vice versa if there is a challenge. Lastly, we come together as a whole class and make our list of "know for sure." The second column is filled with the things we thought we knew but are not so certain of. It's from the second column that we generate questions we'll seek to find answers for.

There's a rationale for each of these steps. Each time students recall information they already have, they are reinforcing that learning. I don't want to reteach or take class time for something the students already know. Generally, whatever the topic, the students collectively bring some knowledge to the class on which we can build. In this manner we are continually moving forward, reinforcing, not reteaching, what is already known. Motivation is higher because students are answering questions they originally posed, not ones the teacher asked them to answer.

Here's the bonus—I don't have to generate all the questions. Remember Alisa's rule about never doing anything the students could and should do. Students are more motivated to answer their own questions, ones they have a genuine interest in, than in answering the teacher's or the textbook's.

Higher Order Thinking Skills

David Thornburg evaluated more than five hundred help-wanted ads in our knowledge-based economy. He compiled those skills most sought after by employers around the world. These are the core skills he identified as necessary for the present-day worker:

1. Digital-Age Literacy: Literacy is not only about reading and writing. Literacy includes knowing how to use a computer, understanding technology, having global awareness. Literacy has a cultural context; what is considered highly literate in an agricultural society is a different literacy than in a technical urban environment.

2. Inventive Thinking: The ability to think outside the box, to take a risk, to seek an alternative solution, is a valued skill. Too often we squash the students who push us beyond our own comfort zone with their creative approaches. We need to encourage rather than discourage alternative problem solving; we should provide time for students to explain how they thought about the problem, how they came to their solutions.

3. Effective Communication: Students need to work in collaborative groups to solve real problems. We need to push them beyond one-word answers. And if we are asking them to talk, then we

need to listen to what they have to say. This doesn't happen overnight, neither for the students nor for the teacher. Students need to develop interpersonal skills; they need training in how to talk to one another in order to enhance learning.

4. High Productivity: Working smarter, not harder is a lesson all teachers should take away as well. Being productive requires knowledge of a wide range of resources, ability to sort through what is valuable and what may not be, and the ability to synthesize information from a variety of sources, print and nonprint.

Considering the rate at which new knowledge is generated and information becomes available (There are more posted web pages than there are people in the world!), educators need to match strategies not only to the content to be taught, but to the skills students need to be successful within and beyond the classroom.

Let's return to the unit on crocodiles for a minute. Suppose, as you are reading the text about crocodiles, you posed these questions: While many reptiles, like the dinosaurs, have become extinct, the crocodile has remained relatively unchanged for millions of years. What about the crocodiles' behaviors has aided their survival? What about human behavior will aid our survival? What might prevent our survival? These are essential questions that stretch the learning and cross disciplines. Questions like these can be explored through multiple lenses throughout the year.

Lessons From the Classroom

A group of teachers who recently participated in a series of workshops around the core propositions concluded their work by trashing some of the classroom activities they had used that hadn't worked. Among those trashed were the following:

- Spending too much time having students take notes and memorize facts for a *fill-in-the-blank* test that had no learning relevance
- Requiring group presentations without providing specific instructions; not requiring sources other than the textbook; and failing to check student work along the way
- Bringing a bad mood to the classroom and using negative consequences when positive reinforcement is much more effective

- Teaching students to check their pulse—everyone said "I have it." On the test they totally bombed. They all had a pulse, but didn't understand what it meant.
- Expecting students to be collaborative at the very beginning of the year—before they knew each other and were able to put their defenses down
- Assigning a project about the revolution that did not require high-enough level thought—basically a pretty timeline
- Trying to get done too fast. Not enough discussion, management, or modeling
And my favorite:
- Turning on the overhead projector just to have a visual. The visual must be relevant and meaningful at that moment, or you lose your audience!

Time is Precious

Everything we do with our students must add value to their lives, build on what they already know, and direct them toward new knowing. To do less is to rob them of the opportunity to learn at high levels.

The Portfolio Entry

The first three portfolio entries in each of the certificate areas direct us to examine our instructional goals. Although the questions vary from certificate to certificate, I've paraphrased some of the portfolio questions to convey their underlying meaning:

- What are your instructional goals for this lesson/unit/activity?
- Why are these appropriate goals for these students at this time?
- How do these assignments assist you in determining your objectives for the next sequence of learning?
- How do these assignments help students to make meaningful connections between what they already know and what they will need to know?

I recently concluded three days of workshops with a group of teachers from our county's court schools. These teachers have very little opportunity for professional development. On the third day I asked them to apply what we had discussed about standards and to write a standards-based lesson appropriate for their teaching assignment. Only then did I understand that they weren't able to articulate their instructional goals. One very conscientious teacher equated instructional goals with the chapter in the textbook and preparation for the end of the chapter short-answer test. He was diligently following the course outline, as he understood it. Reading a chapter may be how you are going to help your students to attain the instructional goal, but it is not the instructional goal. An important instructional goal might be student understanding that the physical earth continually changes through volcanic eruptions, tectonic plate movement, and other environmental factors. The goal is not mastering the unit test. Accomplished teachers know, and are able to articulate to students, and in their National Board portfolio entry, the take-away understandings they want their students to have.

Several entries ask why the topics you've chosen are important for students to know. To assist you, the NB has included, in the *Making Good Choices* section of the portfolio instructions, excerpts from the national content standards to help guide your decision making. The instructions also include some sample strategies. These are not to be construed as requirements for a successful portfolio entry. They are guides, suggestions, examples only, just as mine are. The National Board process is not prescriptive. Each classroom has its own context known best by the teacher. Accomplished teachers have a plan, know the direction in which they want to move their students, and then guide them in that direction. The National Board asks only that you explain your reasoning.

Core Proposition 3

Teachers Are Responsible for Managing and Monitoring Student Learning

Before launching into a discussion of Core Proposition 3, it is important to remind the reader that each proposition is intricately interwoven with the other propositions. Separating them is informative, but in some ways it is also artificial. The propositions overlap, are intertwined, are dependent on one another. You can't break out a proposition and say, if you do this you are an accomplished teacher. You need to provide evidence of all the propositions as they translate into each certificate's standards.

The certificate standards, likewise, do not stand alone. They are not simply a restatement of the core propositions, even though we find each of the five core propositions within the certificate standards. The standards are the application of the propositions addressed within the individual certificate. Therefore, our discussion around core proposition 3 is written based on the assumption that the interested teacher has already read the discussions of the first two propositions and understands that this third discussion is an add-on to what has gone before, not a stand-alone. Effort will be taken to guide the reader through these areas of overlap.

Whereas core proposition 2 emphasized content area knowledge and ways of understanding and teaching the various disciplines, core proposition 3 addresses generic pedagogies, multiple strategies or "tools of the trade" one can call upon when working with distinct groups of students. Making the right connection between the instructional goals for the particular content and the correct strategy for this group of students, or this individual student, at this time, depends also on an understanding of the student as an individual learner—addressed in detail in core proposition 1.

We examine the core propositions individually as a way of organizing the extremely complex tasks that together make up the art and craft of teaching. Later on, when you begin to examine the standards for your certificate area, knowing the core propositions will provide a frame on which to hang still another way of looking at teaching, through the National Board standards.

One of the teacher groups I've worked with described this proposition as an elegant web, all parts woven and dependent upon every other part.

Key Point: Broad Range of Teaching Strategies

A student teacher, after observing my classes for several days, commented that she had recorded at least thirty-seven different strategies I had used with my five classes of students. She then proceeded to read the list from her notes: whip-around, read around, homogeneous groups, student-selected grouping, reciprocal reading, KWL (described in Chapter 3), questioning, Socratic seminar, journaling three different ways, recall, and more. While some strategies were deliberately chosen, I admitted to being hardly aware of having consciously selected several of them. They just seemed a natural choice in response to the teachable moments.

When she expressed concern that she would ever be as knowledgeable or be able to transition so smoothly from one to another, I assured her that I wasn't born knowing all the strategies I'd modeled. Many I learned by attending workshops; others came from observing how students learn, what they respond to, what they do naturally. The general consensus is that it takes five to eight years to master the art and craft of teaching. Whenever I observe another teacher, novice or veteran, I look for what is working well and what I can import into my own classroom. My student teacher and I did discuss, at some length, a teachable moment, a detour from the lesson plan, that nearly got me into trouble.

The principal and the school's mentor teacher coordinator advised me they would be visiting one of my classes to determine if I would be renewed as a mentor teacher for another year. I submitted a lesson plan as instructed, with every intention of following the plan as written. I began the class by reading a Rachel Carson essay. I modeled reading the first paragraph, had students read silently to themselves, then called on volunteers to read the same passage a second time aloud. After reading the first page, students stopped to underline words that were calling to them (I learned this strategy, Call of the Words, at the California Writing Project.). One ninth-grade student spontaneously said that the words, even though they were in a science essay on the environment, sounded poetic. I abandoned the lesson plan at that point, preferring to write poetry using the words the students said called to them. The resulting poems were powerful. Students wrote about their first day of school, about the unknown, about ways of seeing—all from an essay about the edge of the sea.

In the postobservation interview, the principal and lead teacher challenged my decision to switch lessons midway. They thought I should have stayed with the written lesson plan. I disagreed, explaining the importance of saluting the teachable moment when it arrives. It was touch and go whether or not my mentor status would be renewed. They didn't think I was a good model for student teachers who were being taught to write, and adhere to, multiple-step lesson plans. I'll let you be the judge.

The point here is that when you have a wide range of teaching tools to call upon, you can use them as the situation requires. It is important, however, to know which strategy fits where, and to keep your mind on the instructional goals. I often make a good choice, but sometimes I don't. I misjudge the students, or don't provide sufficient instruction or modeling. Knowing when to quit is about as important as knowing which strategy to apply when. If a lesson is going poorly, stop and regroup. Don't be afraid to say to students—this is not working, or I know a better way, or even let's try this new approach. The goal is to provide a learning environment that allows students to take risks. Taking risks means you sometimes make mistakes—even teachers occasionally bomb. The more strategies you know, the more easily you can move between them, sequence them in a meaningful manner, and apply specific strategies to specific situations.

Key Point: Collaboration and Collegiality

I have the wonderful job of working with hundreds of pre-K–12 teachers every year. I prepare for every workshop knowing that I'll learn something during the workshop, usually from one of the teacher participants, sometimes from a copresenter, that I didn't know or hadn't applied before. I'm continually in the position of learning along with teaching. When I had young students, as opposed to the adult students I have now, they also taught me something every day. Be receptive, welcome learning wherever it comes. Everyone has something to offer. When I use a strategy or model I learned from another teacher, I acknowledge where the idea came from. Everyone likes to be given credit for something they devised or improved on. Teachers get so little recognition, it's especially important to acknowledge them—to honor our colleagues.

The days of working in isolation should be over. There's a new breed of educators entering the classroom and they are expecting a collaborative workplace environment. They're referred to as midcareer teachers whose average age is in the early thirties. They come from business and industry where collaboration is a given. They also expect differentiated pay and a career ladder as well as a supportive workplace. We should embrace them. We've been in isolation, living in the egg crate–design factory school for more than a hundred years; it's time to break out.

Elementary teachers are doing a much better job of working in grade-level teams than are secondary teachers. Barriers must still be broken down, especially when it comes to interdisciplinary instruction. The last four years I taught were as part of a three-teacher team: English Language Arts, Integrated Science, and Careers/Technology. The joy of teaching was enhanced through our collaboration. The students benefited because everything they did was reinforced in the other two classes. Schedules were flexible, sometimes one period long, sometimes two-hour blocks. Assignments always covered more than one discipline. There was no downside to our team-teaching arrangement. I recently planned a workshop for teachers in our county-run schools. I called in two other colleagues, Shelia Sutton and Heidi Bowton, one a National Board candidate-in-waiting, and the other an NBCT (National Board Certified Teacher), to assist in writing the curriculum. Together we developed a series of workshops far better than anything we'd have created writing solo. I wouldn't have it any other way. If you're not already working with your colleagues, think of ways to incorporate cross-grade, or interdisciplinary, teaching.

Key point: Collaboration is Valued

National Board portfolio entry 4 in each certificate is about work you do beyond your classroom. Working with colleagues is an integral part of being a professional. Do you attend or conduct workshops sharing best practices? Do you meet in the cafeteria to discuss student work? Have you shared lesson plans—those that worked and those that didn't? Networking is encouraged, whether it's formal or casual. Working in professional learning communities—small groups of teachers focused on improving student achievement—enriches all participants while it cuts through the isolation of the classroom. Without our colleagues' input it would be easy to pass the week without ever speaking meaningfully to another adult educator. As you prepare for National Board Certification think about ways you can open your classroom doors and welcome colleagues to share the professional journey with you.

Key point: Empowering Students

If you're a veteran teacher with many years of experience, making the shift from giver of knowledge to facilitator of learning may be difficult, but it is certainly a worthwhile transition. What will our students need to know and be able to do when they leave our classrooms to enter their work and living communities? The positions they will hold may not even be invented yet. It is our responsibility to prepare them for a future where most will have more than three major career changes in their working lives. The task seems greater than any education system can accomplish. Yet, that's our challenge—to prepare our students for their future, which will not look like our past. Teaching is not about which facts we put into their heads, but about implanting the seeds for their development as lifelong learners. In order to do this successfully it is imperative that we offer ourselves as models of lifelong learners.

NB portfolio entry 4, in addition to requiring you to document your accomplishments with your colleagues, asks that you record what you have done over the previous five years to continue your own professional growth. What have you done? Do you read books about instruction? Research? Assessment? Do you subscribe to and read journals in your field? Do you attend classes? Participate in discussion groups? Belong to professional book clubs? Study student work to improve your teaching and learning? We can't teach students what we don't practice ourselves. Lifelong learning is critical for the worker who will be transitioning from career to career. How do you prepare your students to ask questions and seek answers?

A teacher I admire greatly, Alfee Enciso, has wall posters liberally displayed in his ninth-grade inner-city classroom. On one wall he celebrates failures. Failure, he tells his students, is about taking risks. In his classroom it's okay to try something and not be successful. For his student body, where appearance and saving face is valued, creating a learning environment where students are empowered to stretch themselves is quite a feat. My yoga teacher encourages us to push ourselves a little further each time we attempt to perfect a posture. Falling over is applauded because it means you went beyond your area of comfort and stretched a little higher, or lower, or farther sideways. Accomplished educators strive to provide an environment where students are encouraged to grow, where the status quo is just a starting point. Every certificate has a standard that addresses the learning environment you establish in your classroom. The learning environment is not just about physical safety—that's a given—it's also about emotional and psychological safety.

Empowering students means a willingness on your part not to be in charge all the time. That doesn't mean anarchy. It does entail choice: accepting more than one way of demonstrating accomplishment of the instructional goals. One of the high schools where I taught was only three miles from my home—not nearly enough time to develop a lesson plan on the way to school. One morning, however, I was in just such a position. I hadn't decided which topics to offer students for their culminating essays. I believed in choice and knew I would have more than one option for the students to select from, I just didn't know what the options would be. Then that little voice in my head, belonging to former colleague Alisa Guthrie, turned up. Let the students decide, it said. In class that morning we had a short discussion about the literature we had finished. Then I posed the question: What themes do you want to explore in your culminating essays? The class generated a list from which students were able to choose themes that were meaningful to them. Student buy-in and motivation were high, the essays were diverse and interesting to read, and many students completed the assignment successfully. The added bonus was that I didn't do all the work, the students contributed. They read the literature, they chose what they wanted to write about, they demonstrated engagement with the reading and with one another's topics. Some essays even challenged ideas I had brought up during the reading. What fun!

Key Point: Learning Can Be Hard Work

We are reminded though that learning is not always fun; often it is difficult and challenging. Athletes wouldn't call training for the marathon fun, but they do it anyway. Likewise there are things we ask of our students that aren't fun but that are the necessary building blocks for further accomplishment. One day I had the opportunity to visit two pre-K classrooms in the same urban school. In one, the four-year-olds were busily coloring handles for the spring baskets they were making. This was an annual activity the whole school engaged in prior to Mother's Day. In the second classroom, the four-year-olds were seated quietly on the floor. Before them were mounds of small colored blocks. The teacher, Steve Hicks, also seated on the floor, was asking the little ones to select the colored block that came next in the sequence. Red, red, blue, red, red, followed by what color, he asked. When he was confident they understood the patterns and had created some of their own, he instructed them to recreate their patterns on the handles of the baskets they were making—the same baskets the students in the first classroom were making.

At their desks, crayons in hand, Steve's students were concentrating, transferring the patterns they had created with blocks to the paper handles before them. Patterns are necessary for reading and math; they help us to predict and project. Steve was preparing his students for more difficult learning. Each activity his students engaged in was carefully constructed to move his students toward higher-order thinking and learning. Steve earned National Board Certification that year and then went on to become Los Angeles County teacher of the year finalist. This was the lesson I wrote about in his letter of recommendation and which the judges said defined accomplished teaching. Everything Steve did in his classroom and all the strategies he employed were chosen to help his students achieve the instructional goals.

Key Point: Learning Is Continuous

Just one comment here from the Thornburg book: "It is no exaggeration to state that the computational power of a musical greeting card exceeds the combined power of all the computers on the planet prior to 1950." Read that line again. Think about what it means and why it matters. What can you teach your students now that will be important to their lives in twenty years? Teach them to learn, to seek understanding, to ask and answer questions. Empower them.

Key Point: Assessment

How do we know what our students know? For many educators testing appears to be the only answer. At a national and state level we spend most of the spring administering standardized tests, comparing our students to a national norm. Accomplished teachers, however, don't wait until final exams or spring testing season to assess what their students know and are able to do, they continually examine their student work in order to monitor student learning and teaching effectiveness. Assessing student work can be formal, as in tests and essays, lab reports, and performance projects. It can also be informal as in asking questions and listening for understanding, building on concepts students understand and reteaching those they haven't yet grasped. In an accomplished teacher's classroom, assessment is ongoing, often invisible. Steve, in the scenario just described, was engaged in assessing his students' understanding of patterns, their ability to predict and recall. He watched for class understanding as well as for individual student mastery. He didn't transition to the next activity, coloring patterns on the paper basket handles, until the students were ready. Assessment should not be reserved only for assigning grades. It should be multifaceted, continuous, and informative.

It's worth considering the difference between formative assessment and summative assessment. We're most familiar with the latter although we do the former all the time. Formative assessments make student thinking and learning visible: asking students how they arrived at their solutions and listening to their responses, requiring a journal of the steps taken for a research paper, assigning students to teach the class and noting what they did, what concepts they grasped and which were still unlearned. Summative assessments, on the other hand, measure what students have learned at the end of a lesson, or unit, or period of time. We usually assign grades based on these assessments. Each has a place. For both, it is extremely important that teachers provide prompt feedback; immediate is good, but not always possible. If you can't return the student work within about forty-eight hours, its value for the student drops dramatically—even while your guilt and the pile of ungraded papers rises. If I couldn't grade their work after school hours, the students and I graded their work in class. Most of the time allowing students to grade one another's work, based on a rubric, and requiring consensus between two or three student assessors, led to greater student improvement than did my green-inked commentary on their papers. Engage students in managing and monitoring their own work. Reading every second or third essay a student completes may be as valuable in advancing student learning as struggling to read every one, and will cut the paper load to a manageable mountain.

I began my teaching career as a secondary Language Arts teacher, buried under mounds of student essays that needed editing, commenting, and grading. I had a system: I corrected one set of papers every night, five nights a week. In class the next day, after I returned the graded assignments, too often I saw students taking their papers, checking the grade posted on the top, then tossing them away without even bothering to read the comments I painstaking wrote in green ink—my ed class instructor told us red ink signaled failure. Determined to work smarter, I thought carefully about every mark I put on their papers. If it didn't move their learning forward, why bother? Before marking the next student paper, ask yourself how this grade, correction, or comment will move the student toward accomplishing the instructional goals. If it won't, then why bother to record it? That's also when I began using student portfolios first as collections of student work, then as evidentiary records of their accomplishments. What might you do; what techniques might you employ to build on what the student has already mastered? Grading and commenting on every paper is not the only way to provide feedback to students.

Examining student work provides us an opportunity to see the results of our teaching and the student learning. This is about examining their work, not to assign a grade, but to discover what they are learning, how effective the teaching is, and what should be retaught, expanded on, or even dropped from the curriculum all together. Here are some good questions to ask yourself as you look at your student work. The questions become even more powerful when a group of teachers collaboratively examine their student work.

- How can your teaching be improved by examining student work?
- What concepts do you need to reteach, or teach better?
- What needs to happen in your classroom to assure that all students can attain a 3 or 4 on a 4-point rubric?
- What do the student responses tell you about the effectiveness of the assignment?
- The clarity of the instructions?

There's an excellent website that focuses on issues surrounding student work: *www.lasw.org*. The more you are able to use your student work to assess your teaching effectiveness, the more you will grow as a professional. Recently a math teacher, a candidate for NB certification, sheepishly admitted to a group of other candidates I support, that her students were doing better since she began paying more attention to the instructions she gave and to her teaching. Teacher quality is the single most important factor in student achievement. We can't say that often enough.

Don't be the judge and jury of student accomplishment. Take student work public. Develop ways for students to share one another's work, to review it, comment on it, grade it against assignment rubrics, and learn from it. Share your students' work by exchanging with other teachers or classes. Students make more effort when they know their audience is greater than the teacher. What would happen if parents and/or school leaders regularly examined your students' work? Chances are you would be more thoughtful in the assignments you gave if you knew other adults would be seeing the resulting student work—students are more careful in responding when they know their work will reach a wide audience, including their parents.

Key Point: Individual and Group Teaching

An essential tension teachers must work with daily is how to teach individual students in a group setting. If we know that not all students learn in the same way, or at the same rate, how do we honor individual differences in a group context? (I'm going to include my email address at the end of the book. If you have a surefire answer, contact me.) To date, no one has devised a method that always works for all classes of students. The best we can do is to try to know each student individually, a major challenge in itself, and continually monitor their progress. Be flexible. Determine when small group assignments are called for and when whole group instruction is more effective.

Research around tracking students into ability-like groupings details and documents its evils, yet low-achieving students, especially at the secondary level, sometimes become complacent when placed with very high achieving students in heterogeneous groups. They've learned the high achievers will do the work. I have found that while I want to have lower-achieving students see high-quality work, I also want to push them individually. I can sometimes do this better in homogeneous groups. The high achievers will run with the assignment, while you will have more time to work with those students who might most benefit from your facilitation and guidance. There will be an expectation that they produce a product without the help of those students who always produce at high levels.

Because there is no one way that is right all the time for every group of students, teachers need to have a big toolbox to draw upon. Teachers need to match strategies to instructional goals and to students. They must constantly evaluate students' work, adjusting, even reversing strategies if students aren't successful—a monumental task that is of critical importance.

Portfolio entries 2 and 3 require a videotape of your classroom instruction. Several certificates call for both a whole group videotape and a small group tape. Are you able to analyze and articulate why you chose each strategy as the best means of accomplishing the instructional goals you set? Do you know what strategy works best in which setting and why? Next time you move the students into groups tell them the reason for that strategy and how it will help them. If you are very fortunate, they'll give you some insight about what is working for them and what isn't. I wish I had asked my students for their thoughts about my teaching more often than once at the end of every semester. They always gave me good information. Some of the lessons I loved, they ignored completely. Others, which I thought were just fill-in, addressed their needs well. Just as it is beneficial to provide a wide audience for student work, so can we benefit by opening our teaching to a wider audience—colleagues, administrators, students, and parents.

Key Point: Classroom Management

New teachers tend to establish complex rules with multilevels of consequences they will apply if students break the rules. I've never had more than three rules: Be prepared, Be prompt, Be polite. That covers it all.

Rule 1—Be prepared: If you come to class unprepared—lacking supplies, or with incomplete assignments—you suffer. I don't give you the supplies you should have brought from home (and which we have determined you have access to, or the school has previously provided). Likewise, if you've chosen to not do the homework, you sit to the side until it's done. The rest of the class is not held back while you do what you should have done before.

Rule 2—Be prompt: Come to class on time. Turn in assignments when they are due. Teachers tend to be great enablers, offering students multiple opportunities for all manner of things. We should provide multiple opportunities for students to master the instructional goals, but that is different from not holding them accountable for meeting deadlines. Employers expect their employees to show up for work on time. We fail to prepare our students for the future when we expect any less.

I have two experiences to share with you. The first occurred when I was consulting at a very low performing inner-city high school. A teacher had asked for assistance and invited me to observe his first-period class. When I arrived five minutes before class was to begin, none of the students had yet entered the room. They dribbled in over the next twenty-five minutes. At 8:20 a bell rang and the missing students poured into class. They had learned that even though the class was supposed to begin at 8:00, the tardy sweep didn't happen until 8:20. Students who arrived on time were actually held back because the teacher repeated instructions every time a student entered the room during the first twenty minutes of class. It was no wonder the school's performance was abysmal. Students learn what we teach them.

Compare that setting with my own classroom. When I taught high school seniors, assignments that were due that day were collected as soon as the bell rang. I taught at five different high schools and because I was frequently new to the school the seniors didn't know at first that I meant what I said. About the third week of school, just as the bell rang, I collected the first major essay, due that day. A student arrived about five minutes into the period, sat down, took out her completed assignment and proceeded to turn it in. I refused to accept it. I told her I had already collected the papers when they were due. Late papers, unless we had a prior arrangement or there were special circumstances, were not accepted. The class gave a collective gasp. I moved on with the day's lesson. There were no late papers in that class for the remainder of the semester. Those students had learned a lesson about expectations in the world beyond the classroom. Of course, if the students weren't seniors, ready to graduate, I might have used a different strategy, but seniors needed to get that message immediately.

Some of my colleagues gasp when I tell this story, because five minutes seem so unimportant. Hear me out on this one. It wasn't about the five minutes, it was about helping the student develop the habit of mind around punctuality. It was also about honoring all the other students who arrived and turned in their work on time. I can't tell you how often I've been in a classroom and watched students fidget as the teacher was extracting an explanation about tardiness or some other infraction from one student. We waste a lot of instructional time talking to the student who is breaking the rules and ignoring the students who are there ready to learn. Many of my students at year-end say they liked my class because they always knew what was expected and that I wanted them to be successful. I think the latter point is the key here. Students need to know you care about them, that your rules aren't capricious and aren't about displaying your power. The senior whose paper wasn't accepted put it in her portfolio to be turned in with her ten-week evaluation. She said that since then she was really working at getting to school on time every day. Sometimes she didn't make it, but she wasn't late as often as she used to be. Long after we forget what the essay assignment was all about, we'll remember the lesson.

Rule 3—Be polite: Call it politeness or respect for others, it means the same thing. I don't speak when students are not listening. I listen when they're talking. The same rule applies to everyone in the class. It works. I also don't use street language and don't tolerate it from the students. A colleague told me that street slang was a way of life in the inner city school where we taught. Not in my class, I said. Students paid $.25 for each foul word they uttered within my hearing. In the course of a semester we never gathered enough quarters to buy a pizza. The students learned that quickly. I learned something also. Most kids don't swear in school. Those who do are loud and often give the impression of being the majority, but they're not. Several students thanked me quietly, usually in one of their journals, for cleaning up the class language. They told me no one cursed in their homes and hearing street words in school was distracting and upsetting. Another stereotype out the window!

Key Point: The Essential Tension

Here's one of the many reasons why I applaud accomplished teachers; they manage to teach to every child in the room as if that child were the only one there. And they do this in classes of thirty-five and more. Children learn one at a time. We need to connect with each one of them. One of the most powerful stories I've ever read was written by a teacher about a student she had. Many of you may know it: "Cipher in the Snow." For those of you who don't know Jean Mizer's true story of the student who just faded out of existence, it is worth reading. In it she writes about a boy who didn't make any impact at school, just collected Ds and sat silently by himself. When he died she asked, "How do you go about making a boy into a zero?" I adopted her challenge as my own. Mizer wrote: "I've never forgotten Cliff Evans nor that resolve. He has been my challenge year after year, class after class. I look for veiled eyes or bodies scrounged into a seat in an alien world. "Look, kids," I say silently. "I may not do anything else for you this year, but not one of you is going to come out of here as a nobody. I'll work or fight to the bitter end doing battle with society and the school board, but I won't have one of you coming out of there thinking himself a zero." I feel like Jean Mizer does when she says: "Most of the time—not always, but most of the time—I've succeeded." There's a little bit of a missionary in every good teacher. You can download the story from : *www.teenlit.com/teachers/cipherin.html.*

Key Points:
- ## Effective Teachers Have a Broad Range of Strategies for Both Assessment and Classroom Management and Know When to Use Them.
- ## Teachers Must Motivate Students, Capture Their Hearts and Minds, and Engage Them Actively in Their Learning.

These two key points are intricately connected; I didn't realize how much until a school asked me to present a workshop on classroom management. I tried and tried to plan the workshop, but I couldn't come up with any classroom management techniques I employed, other than the three preceding rules, which were stand-alones. Everything I did, from how portfolios were kept and groups assigned, was intricately connected to the teaching strategies, which in turn were connected to the content and instructional goals, in a continuous feedback loop. When students are engaged in their learning, they manage themselves. A quiet, orderly classroom doesn't mean that learning is happening and neither does a noisy disorganized one. If we shift from classroom management to student engagement, we can provide evidence of both.

All teachers should have a solid understanding of how people learn. There are many great books available; browse the web and select your favorite. I like one called *How People Learn* (ISBN 0-309-07036-8). One of the principal contributors is Lee Shulman of the Carnegie Foundation—principal author of the National Board Standards. With every page I read I yelled eureka! Everything I had been reading and applying from the core propositions is based on solid research around how people learn.

We learn based on what we already know, and children know a lot more than we give them credit for. We learn in a social context within the zone of proximal development (Vygotsky). That means we can learn something that's a little bit of a challenge, just enough to cause some tension, but not so much as to cause too much stress. If it's too much of a challenge, most of us won't try. If there's a little gap, we're motivated to bridge it. Effective teachers provide just the right amount of scaffolding and modeling to help students acquire more knowledge.

Students are more motivated to learn if they can see the results of their learning. In my practice, nothing motivated students more than providing the time to analyze their portfolios every few weeks. I asked them to select a piece of work they did at the beginning of the time period and redo it, then write about how they came to know more than they knew just weeks before. The next questions were about how they were going to continue to learn by the next portfolio examination. I stumbled across this technique when I was working with Secondary English Language Learners. They start the school year very enthusiastically, but by December they hit a low. They know enough English to want to really engage in conversation, but not enough to do so easily. I'd have the students pull some work from September or October and examine what they knew then, how little English. Then we'd talk about how much they had learned in the past few months and set some goals for the months ahead. It never failed to lift their spirits and get them motivated to work even harder. I didn't offer any gold stars or chocolate bars or game time. All I offered was more work, and they rose to the challenge. Learning is motivating. Knowing is motivating. Being able to do that which you've set out to do, raises your self-esteem. Voilà! Classroom management.

Core Proposition 4

Teachers Think Systematically About Their Practice and Learn From Experience

It seems appropriate, since this core proposition focuses on reflective practice, to begin the chapter with a reflection. Take a few moments to write about the following:

- Consider the role of reflection in your professional life.
- Consider the role of reflection in the lives of your students.
- How might our lives, and the lives of our students, be enhanced through time for reflection about learning?
- How do you or could you allow for reflective time, for yourself and your students, in your classroom practice?

While preparing to write this chapter—rereading the core propositions, thinking about my past and current teaching—my mind has been wandering. And it's been wondering about the wandering. Where do teachers find time to allow their minds to wander? Is it in the midst of teaching or receiving thirty-plus youngsters each period, or having little hands waving in their face calling, Me, me, me? Is it driving home at the end of day? Perhaps it's just before dozing off at night. Or maybe during journal writing. Reflective time, time set aside to think about the day's or week's events, is a gift you give yourself, and a gift you can give to your students.

One Friday afternoon when I was teaching ninth-graders, the lesson was over ten minutes before the bell was scheduled to ring, not enough time to begin something new, too much time to waste. I quickly instructed my students to open their journals and write about something they had learned during the past week. I, of course, was expecting them to write about what they had learned in our English Language Arts class, but although everyone wrote, almost no one wrote about our class. They wrote feverishly, every student filled a page, even the usually reluctant ones. They wrote about how many times you could flip a penny and still have the same number of heads and tails. One student wrote about a conversation he'd had with his mother about growing up. They wrote about someone they'd learned to trust, and someone else who wasn't trustworthy. One wrote a mini-essay about how homework was ruining the time he spent with his family, something that was on his mind. The point here is that every student welcomed the opportunity to think and write about their learning. I didn't even know the word *metacognition* at the time, but that's what was happening—thinking about thinking and learning.

One of the many strengths of the National Board process is its expectation that accomplished teachers are reflective about their practice. National Board Certification is not a diploma signifying that you now know it all; *au contraire*. National Board Certification is achieved by accomplished teachers who are continually improving their practice because they don't know it all, they don't have all the answers to this most complex of endeavors. After all, "The normal condition of the mind," according to *flow* expert Mihaly Csikszentmihalyi, "is one of informational disorder: random thoughts chas[ing] one another instead of lining up in logical causal sequences." He warns, "Unless one learns to concentrate, and is able to invest the effort, thoughts will scatter without reaching any conclusion" (p. 29). It is only after the experience, when we take the time to look back on what has happened, that we are able to understand the teaching moment, what it meant, and why it may or may not matter.

The key points in this fourth National Board core proposition serve as a model for what reflective practice looks like. I've pulled them apart and treated them separately, but like the core propositions themselves, the separation is artificial; in reality they overlap, are intertwined, feed and inform one another. Keep that in mind as you continue reading.

Key Point: Continual Professional Development

We improve our practice by keeping abreast of classroom-related research. We read in our content areas, learn new strategies, deepen our understanding of how children and adults learn. We study journal articles, participate in workshops, and attend conferences. We learn from our colleagues. We listen to our students' thinking. Through formal and informal community partnerships, we bring parents and workers, artists and business professionals into our classrooms, and we go to theirs. We are observers of life, passionate about the world. We ask questions of everyone, frequently challenge the texts we read, question the motives and perceptions of others, all in an effort to deepen our own understanding. We model the lifelong learning we want for our students. Our union contracts may designate set teaching hours, but accomplished teachers are never off duty.

Prior to becoming an educator I spent twenty years working in the business community, as an entrepreneur and a corporate executive. I incorporated those years of experience into my classroom practice, and again into my professional development work with adults. I continue to read business journals, frequently pulling paradigms from marketing and management into my work as an educator. Commercial markets have to be sensitive to clients' needs. Successful businesspeople are problem solvers. As educators we should pay more attention to our clients, the students, and to their problems. I was surprised when I first began teaching that my school wasn't asking: How can we best meet the needs of the children in this community? At this school? How can we develop relationships that encourage and support lifelong learning? I'm still asking those questions.

Professional development is continuous and happens in a variety of settings, some not directly related to education. During a visit to an art museum a docent, speaking about the artist's efforts and vision, said his paintings converted abstract ideas and feelings into concrete images. Poetry does that also, I remember thinking. Following that Saturday afternoon museum experience I revised my poetry unit to begin with helping students transform their abstract ideas and feelings into concrete images.

I continue to learn from a variety of settings. I want to return to Csikszentmihalyi because he says it more succinctly than I can: "First, one must pay attention so as to understand thoroughly what is happening and why; second, it is essential not to accept passively that what is happening is the only way to do the job; then one needs to entertain alternatives and to experiment with them until a better way is found" (p. 105). That docent revealed more than what the artist had accomplished, she opened a new lens through which I might look at poetry; something I could take back to my teaching practice. I realized that not one of my English classes in high school or college had ever helped me to make that connection between the abstract and the concrete. Teaching, no matter how proficient, is always a work in progress. And so is learning.

Key Point: Difficult Choices

Teaching is complex, and fertile ground for generating numerous tensions. There's tension in teaching the individual in the context of the group. There's pressure to satisfy the demand for improved standardized test scores; to devote time for in-depth concept development even when it means sacrificing total coverage. There's the tension that arises when you provide time for youngsters to make mistakes, to seek answers, to pose questions that push their thinking beyond the boundaries of the text book. Sadly, many teachers, wonderfully effective teachers, are leaving urban classrooms where decisions have been made to adopt scripted reading and math programs that may not meet the needs of all youngsters; in some contexts the tension is simply too great between doing what is required and doing what is best for students. Still others resolve the conflict by adding what the script doesn't address. How one resolves or learns to live with the many tensions inherent in teaching, affects our effectiveness. Sometimes I wish there were one answer or method, other times I celebrate the diversity inherent in teaching. Nevertheless, new tensions arrive every day.

How do we replenish ourselves when teaching requires so much energy? Noted author Donald Graves' provides one answer in his book *The Energy to Teach*. To discover where and how teachers replenish their energy Graves traveled across the country asking teachers the following question: What gives you energy, what takes energy away, and what, for you, is a waste of time? This is a great question to ask yourself. There are colleagues at your school site who are a joy to be around. They genuinely enjoy teaching; they share lessons; they tell stories about their students' mishaps and triumphs and throw in a few about themselves. An hour with them feels like five minutes and leaves you refreshed and renewed. Then there are the *others*. Teachers who walk around with long faces; who talk about *those students* and how *those students aren't like my former students*. They complain, they take from you without ever giving back. They are an endless drain on your energy. Graves suggests that you avoid them and spend more time with the people and activities that restore and replenish you. Apply the same criterion to the committee meetings you're attending and everything else you do around the school. Find what serves the students and also suits you—then do it.

Here's a rule of thumb to go by: How does this person, or this activity, impact student learning? If the answer is not at all, then you may want to consider dropping that person or activity from your must-see or must-do list.

Do consider people and activities outside of yourself, but don't discount the impact on your students of yourself as a model. According to Graves, "It is the quality of our own lives as we engage with the world that is one of the major sources of energy for our students. It is the questions you ask aloud about the world, your curiosity, the books you read, and your personal use of writing that teach far more than any methodological course you've ever taken. . . You, the teacher, are the most important condition in the room" (p. 35). That's an awesome responsibility.

Making good choices is also about choosing. The NB instructions specifically ask you to make choices about what you will feature in your portfolio entries. The entries are a slice of your practice, not the whole practice, and it is important that you choose well. More about that when we talk about the entries later on.

Key Point: Lifelong Learning

For however many years you teach, the one certainty is that you'll never do it perfectly. Everything and everyone has the power to influence our teaching practices. Each student and each class informs and changes us. The information researchers uncover about how we learn, even each wave of the political will, presents the possibility of undoing what we've done before. That's the dilemma of teaching—that there's no one way to do it right—and that's also the challenge and the excitement. It's what draws us back into the classroom day after day—to solve the problem posed the lesson or the week or the youngster before. How to encourage lifelong learning, young people excited about discovery, willing to try things they haven't tried before? How best to prepare them, and ourselves, to be lifelong learners?

How does what you do in the classroom, the choices you make, help students to acquire the skills they will need to be productive members of society? (We are back to the subject of making good choices.)

In our quest to do it right we have to spend time thinking about what we're doing. It's not the experiences we have as teachers that continually inform and improve our practices, it's thinking about those experiences.

Key Point: Learning From Experience

What do you think about when you look at your student's work? For most of us, we look at our students' work in order to assign grades. Sometimes our immediate goal is to assist students with revising their essays, or with recalculating their math problems. More rarely do we examine student work with the goal of improving our own teaching.

Take another few moments to respond to one or more of the following sentence starters as fully and as honestly as possible. For this reflection it may be helpful to visualize a particular student's work, or a set of student responses to a recent assignment. Even better, pull a stack of papers before you as you answer this prompt. (I promise you I'm not straying from the core propositions.)

When I look at student work:

- I expect . . .
- I see . . .
- I assume . . .
- I learn . . .
- I fear . . .
- I have doubts about . . .
- I am disappointed in . . .
- I become . . .
- I celebrate . . .
- I want to change . . .
- I want to expand upon . . .
- I am frustrated by . . .
- And . . .

What would you have to do differently to help your students produce work that meets the course objectives, earns a 3 or 4 on a 4-point rubric, and that is also important for them to know within and beyond the school-house doors? What are the challenges or barriers to your doing that (whatever that is)? What is the risk in abandoning something you've done in the past that wasn't effective, or no longer meets students' needs? What are the possible benefits? I had a recent personal setback in my consulting work. I presented a plan for professional development to an underperforming school district and was turned down. They elected to remain with their current professional development provider, even though the workshops they offered were not very effective and hadn't impacted the classrooms. The district said they didn't want to confuse the teachers by making a change. I have never had the experience of my clients, young students or adult learners, feeling confused when we changed strategies. If the first wasn't effective, they welcomed the change. But change is difficult and involves risk. The school district wasn't ready to take the risk.

If you haven't already read it (or seen the delightful little film with the same name), I recommend the book by Dr. Johnson, *Who Moved My Cheese?* He reminds us that change happens and that the quicker you let go of old cheese (or ineffective teaching practices) the sooner you can enjoy new cheese.

Effective teaching is about growing and learning, about thinking critically and analyzing the outcomes of your teaching. It's about thinking about what we do, analyzing and reflecting upon it continuously—not just at the end of the summer in preparation for the new semester. Teachers are classroom-based action researchers, even though most of us never publish our findings. We develop and design, implement, evaluate, and refine our lessons. We are constantly on the lookout for ways to engage students in their own learning. We think about what we do and ask students to do the same. We're not afraid to admit we made a mistake.

See if you can top this goof. A second-grade teacher invited a different community helper to address her class each week. A neighborhood librarian, a mail carrier, a firefighter, and a sanitation engineer were all guest speakers—without a hitch. The children were especially excited when the sheriff arrived. He gave his talk and responded to the six-year-olds' questions. Perhaps to make up for their disappointment that he hadn't worn his gun he invited all the students outside to see the bus the sheriff's department used to transport inmates. The kids eagerly scampered aboard the blue bus with the barred windows. They had a great time—learning all the new words the inmates had scratched on the walls and seats! More than one angry parent called the next day. The teacher learned how important it is to preview lesson materials, all of them. She goofed, but she learned and she won't make the mistake of assuming her guests would have thought through all the implications of their presentations. She's the expert in children, not they.

Give yourself permission to make mistakes, but learn from them. Share them with your students and they will learn also. You'll also be a model to help students learn from their own experiences. That's what lifelong learning is about.

Key Point: Domesticating versus Liberating Education

One of the most powerful books I've ever read about teaching is Patrick Finn's *Literacy With an Attitude* (1999). In it he builds upon Chilean educator Pablo Fiere's work educating the working class. I bring it up now because much of what we are asked to teach in this age of accountability, as measured by standardized tests, goes against what we know to be dynamic teaching for lifelong learning. Domesticating education, according to Finn, provides minimal literacy and prepares students for low-skill jobs. It is characterized by overreliance on strategies like these:

- Knowledge taught is not related to the lives and experiences of the students.
- Teachers do not make a practice of explaining how assignments are related to one another.
- Students' access to materials (and information) is tightly controlled.

Contrast that with liberating or empowering education—the kind of education our nation's future leaders receive:

- Discussion of challenges to the status quo, past and present, frequently occurs.
- Textbook knowledge is validated or challenged in terms of knowledge gained from experience.
- Students are rewarded for initiative and inquisitiveness, not passivity and obedience.

What do you do if your school awards teachers whose classes are quiet and orderly with students busily filling out worksheets or bubbling Scantrons to practice test taking? Effective teaching takes energy, and it also takes courage to do what you believe is best for students.

The National Board portfolio guiding questions ask for your instructional goals. To meet the NB standards you not only have to be articulate about your goals, but know why they are the appropriate goals for your students at this time. Accomplished teachers carefully select the strategies to employ and know why those are the right strategies for this content with this group of students at this time. Accomplished teachers are ready to explain their choices to anyone who asks.

Here's another caveat: we run the risk of *falling in love* with our own choices. Remember that the proof of effectiveness is not in the teaching, but in the students' learning. (I'm reminded of the teacher who told me that he'd been teaching this lesson for twenty years and it was the students' fault they didn't get it!) Don't be the teacher who complains for twenty years that the students aren't getting it. If they aren't, what do you have to do differently so they do? If challenged, do you have evidence the strategy you've chosen to teach this material is effective with your students? Does what you do help students to accomplish the important instructional goals you've set for them?

My choices have been challenged by administrators, parents, and even by students, more than a few times during my career. I always answer the challenges by referring to the evidence—the student work (that's only one of the reasons why I'm such a fan of student portfolios). Usually, once we sit and examine the evidence together, we collectively agree that the opportunity to learn was provided in an effective, supportive manner. Once in a while, we discover some flaws in the teaching, and I learn from them. The National Board is not your adversary, but they do ask that you provide evidence that what you're doing in your classroom results in helping students move toward accomplishing the instructional goals—an essential question we should be continually asking ourselves.

Key Point: Educators as Moral Beings

Whether we consciously elected to be role models for our students or not, we are. Teachers do have a greater responsibility to act in a moral manner when we are publicly observed and even when we aren't. We must treat all students with dignity, respect their diverse cultures, honor the cultural literacy and knowledge they bring to class with them. If we want all students to learn at high levels, we have to learn at high levels and share the adventure of being a knowledge-seeker with them. It is our charge to educate a population to understand our democratic principles and be capable of upholding them. We must be tolerant, respect multiple viewpoints, be fair and just with all our students—and with our colleagues. Our students trust us. We betray that trust when we behave in a manner that is below the community standard of morality. The whole profession suffers when a teacher is charged with illegal or immoral behavior. We must first be vigilant about ourselves, and then about our colleagues.

Last weekend I saw one of my former students busing tables at the restaurant where my husband I were dining. The former student told me he'd started college but did more partying than studying. After two semesters he dropped out, but was returning in the fall—a lot wiser and more motivated. A few days later I recognized a hospital worker as another former student. We sat and chatted for a long time. He told me how ten years earlier my pushing him affected his life and how he wished he'd pushed himself harder. He was thrilled that I was back in graduate school, even at my advanced age, because he'd returned to college, at age thirty, to finish his bachelor's degree and wasn't sure he was doing the right thing. We are eternally models for our students.

Society may have come a long way since the time it demanded female teachers remain single, pure, and completely dedicated to their students. Nevertheless, society still has higher moral expectations for teachers than it does for other public figures (think politicians, business leaders, and sports figures). I agree with the National Board that we should hold ourselves to a higher standard.

Key Point: Reflective Nature

Some of us are more reflective by nature than others. I was fortunate in this area. A severe speech defect as a child was the impetus for my writing more than speaking. In elementary school my speech was so slurred I seldom raised my hand; I kept my counsel to myself and recorded my thoughts in a series of journals. I continue to maintain a personal journal and have boxes filled with them. For those of you who do not regularly reflect, you can learn. Once you set aside a fixed time every day or week, the habit of reflection will follow you everywhere. Here's a simple exercise to get started. (If you've been doing the suggested reflections as you are reading this book, you've already begun.)

At the end of the day, or week write down something you did or said in class. Apply the Say—Mean—Matter technique from Chapter 1. In a few lines write down what you did or said. Follow that with a few more lines about what you meant, your reasons for the behavior. Finally, think about why it mattered, or why it continues to matter. That's the reflective piece.

Example

Say/Do: One day in my English 9B class I returned a set of papers telling the students that it was a pretty sorry set of essays, but that it was mostly my fault for not teaching the concept very well. I asked them if I retaught the lesson, would they be willing to redo the essay. Relieved, they agreed.

Mean: This meant that they would have another chance at demonstrating mastery of this concept, allied to a required standard about analysis. It also meant that I would have another opportunity to teach the concept. It meant we were a community of learners; it wasn't me against them.

Matter: This experience mattered a great deal. First, the students weren't blamed for poor performance, and they really appreciated that. As the teacher, I accepted responsibility for not having done my job well enough for the students to master the target skill. The students learned that even a teacher could mess up by not teaching a great lesson, and then recover. It's better to confess to a poor performance than try to cover up and bury yourself deeper. This last may have been the most important lesson for the students and me.

You'll notice as you read this very brief example, that *mean* and *matter* are closely aligned. That's because analysis and reflection are not so easy to separate, nor is it necessary to do so. The important thing here is to think through what you do, determine if the impact or the effect is a positive one or not. If not, don't do it again. That's what the core proposition means: *Teachers think systematically about their practice and learn from experience.*

Core Proposition 5

Teachers Are Members of Learning Communities

5

This core proposition speaks to our work, and our students' learning, within and beyond the classroom. Our profession can no longer maintain the myth that students primarily learn while in school. Actually, only about 14 percent of what students learn occurs in school, and even some of that small percentage is happening away from teachers. Our students learn from parents, from one another, from television, and from being teenagers and thinking about their experiences. We can continue to teach in a relative vacuum, following the tradition of isolationism, leaving much of learning to random events, or we can engage the entire community in providing meaningful learning experiences for our children. This core proposition restates the ancient African proverb: It takes a village to raise a child.

Although teaching is the "daily conduct of lessons" it extends well beyond the classroom door. It is no longer acceptable for teachers and teaching to remain isolated in and limited to individual classrooms. It is past time to break down the symbolic walls of the schoolhouse, wherein each classroom and teacher remain within an egg crate–like structure originally designed to discourage teacher collaboration and prevent the combining of disciplinary instruction. The world our educated students will enter is not defined by the assembly-line factory, and neither should the way we teach artificially separate disciplines and grade levels from one another. Unfortunately, many teachers, myself included, earned our credentials from professors whose own schooling was based on the factory model. We tend to be most comfortable teaching the way we learned, or the way we thought we learned. Fortunately, many of the midcareer teachers now entering the profession are bringing new paradigms from their prior work experiences. They seek out collaborative learning environments. They search for team teaching partners. They open their classroom doors, welcoming opportunities for observation and demonstration. Often, our newest teachers, especially the change-of-career folk, bring to their classrooms a greater knowledge of the business community than many of us have. We can capitalize on their experiences by making connections to the world beyond the schoolhouse.

Attending to students' intellectual growth is only part of the school's job. Because of our ever more diverse student population and their expectation that more of their needs will be addressed in the school setting, we need to reach out and extend teaching and learning to embrace families and the community-at-large as partners. Where to start?

Key Point: Teachers Work Collaboratively With One Another

Start here, with your colleagues and with the administrators at your school site. Examine the school data. What does it say about student learning? About the education level and preparedness of the faculty and staff? What human, physical, and financial resources are available? How are decisions about curriculum and instruction made and by whom? These are all essential questions to inform our practice. By our practice I'm referring to the work of the full school community, not just what an individual teacher does.

Traditionally, teachers were expected to follow orders and deliver the curriculum and instruction dictated by administrators. The times are changing. Administrators can't, and shouldn't, be expected to determine best practices for students. In more and more settings teachers are invited to work with administrators and district personnel to determine curriculum, select materials, and investigate strategies that are most effective for their students. This is happening in schools all across the country. I also know that in many districts, especially urban districts with large percentages of underperforming schools and students and many underprepared teachers, teachers are expected to follow proprietary scripts for reading and math instruction. This is another of today's tensions in education. Collectively we can work towards reversing this trend. Those of us who are closest to students need to be making more of the curricula decisions. But our decisions, and here's where we've been weak in the past, need to be based on a combination of the best available research in learning and teaching and careful collection and analysis of student-generated data.

Accomplished teachers working alongside colleagues and administrators determining what constitutes valuable learning and how best to teach so students can learn is a powerful model. In making decisions the broad school community recognizes the country, state, and district's mandates as well as the literacies valued by their students' community. Curriculum is not static, neither is it reactive. Curriculum evolves to best prepare students for success in the economic, civic, and personal worlds they will inhabit. While we should be working more collaboratively, let's not confuse collaboration with continual agreement. Sometimes we disagree about what is important for students to know and be able to do. Working collaboratively means presuming positive intentions, respecting one another's diverse opinions, and then working to assure students benefit from our decisions. The students' needs, not our personal agendas, should determine the actions taken.

Determinations about student outcomes should be based on helping students to fulfill university and postsecondary school entry-level requirements, an awareness of the needs of the larger community, trends in global economic development, and advances in technology that will alter our students' lives beyond our wildest imaginings.

Collaboration can be as official as serving on textbook adoption committees and as unofficial as lesson planning over lunch. I was fortunate in that my first teaching assignment was in a high school whose English department was highly collaborative. We met weekly during lunchtime expressly to share lesson plans and the student work that resulted from those lessons. Indeed, I thought this type of collaboration was the norm, and am still saddened that it is not.

Collaboration requires interpersonal skills, knowing how to work on a team toward a common goal. I learned through my experiences conducting National Board support programs that just because we are educated adults doesn't mean we know how to work well together. While assisting candidates with the NB process my candidate groups spend time learning how to work together in professional communities. These are skills, once learned, that are important for us to teach our students as well.

Key Point: Breaching the Boundaries

During the past hundred-plus years of public education, we've been highly successful at building artificial boundaries between grade levels, disciplines, and specializations. Science teachers (can't, don't, won't, seldom—you pick) teach math. Secondary language arts teachers don't teach reading. Fourth-grade teachers don't know the fifth-grade curriculum, or the third-. The world beyond the schoolhouse door is not divided into disciplines and grade levels as neatly as is the world within. Indeed, it is not divided along these lines at all. As accomplished educators we can best serve our students by providing an interdisciplinary curriculum that is complex and diverse and transfers across grade levels and beyond the schoolhouse doors.

Teaching for maximum student learning is not the private reserve of teachers, or even of schools. Welcoming the community and students' families as teaching partners, each encouraged to bring their expertise, enriches our students' experiences. The National Board does not prescribe any specific ways to engage communities and families in student learning, nor does it sponsor any business associations that work with schools. That said, there are some strategies and organizations that are especially effective in enriching student learning. The following ideas are based on my experiences and those of the teachers I have worked with throughout the last dozen years. They are offered because it's not productive for each of us to reinvent teaching.

Service learning is a wonderful strategy that connects students to the community and engages their need to be productive, to make a difference, and to contribute. Service learning differs from community service in substantive ways. For many students community service begins with a school, church, or family requirement that they expend X number of unpaid hours as a volunteer in a nonprofit setting. Service learning, on the other hand, begins with the identified needs of some segment of the community and builds curriculum around satisfying that need. The food drive serves as a good example.

Community Service

In this model students conduct a food drive at school or in their neighborhood. The donated food then goes to a food bank. Often the donated items consist of food no one wants and are frequently past their best use dates. Success is measured by the number of items collected and redistributed, not by how well the food served the needs of the community.

Service Learning

A community-based food bank either approaches the school for assistance or is solicited by the school as a possible recipient for a service learning project. The food bank's needs are evaluated. Students collectively consider the people to be served, the total number of meals wanted. In health class students study the nutritional requirements for a healthy life. In social studies/history class they learn about the clients' cultural food preferences. In home economics they develop menus and cook sample meals. In math they study weights and measures, determining the necessary quantities for each item on the menus they developed. They solicit specific food items from the school and neighborhood. Their government class learns about government programs they might contact to help them. Once the food is collected, students arrange for transportation, learning about costs, refrigeration needs, and working with businesses. In the best service learning activities students work in several different disciplines toward completing this service learning project. Service learning is about more than the students or school doing something for the community-based organization, because the project grows from the organization's specific needs. Throughout the project the target organization is working with the school to engage students in a rich, real-world learning experience.

Service learning projects can be massive, spanning the whole school community and school year, or completed by a single class in a limited amount of time. Where there is extensive collaboration, the experience engages the imagination and interest of the school community. Students feel good, and learn by doing for others. These are experiences that enrich their lives forever. In 1990 President George Bush signed the National and Community Service Act defining service learning. We learn only 5 percent of what we hear in a lecture, but retain more than 75 percent of what we practice and 90 percent of what we teach others. There are no downsides to service learning.

A service learning project a science teacher and I conducted with our students continues to enrich the school. Our combined classes built a science pond at the school to enhance the department's ability to teach environmental science. Our students selected the site, determined the necessary materials, raised money to purchase supplies, and built the pond, mostly after school and on the weekends. Several families came to school and mixed cement alongside the students. Because there would not be a pump the pond had to be perfectly balanced. Students calibrated the number of fish to the number and types of plants. Then they stocked the pond. Once the pond was completed, they continued to sample the water and maintain its ecological balance. There was an unexpected side benefit as well. During every nutrition and lunch break several students policed the area. They made certain no one used the pond for trash, or desecrated the pond or its fish and plant life in any way. In addition to everything they learned about ecology, they also developed pride in their work and in their school. What they did meant something to others besides themselves.

In addition to breaching class levels and disciplines, we need more collaboration between the classroom teacher and social service providers. The school nurse, psychologist, and counselors should be part of the students' team. Call upon the librarian, the resource and special education teachers. Classroom teachers have the most contact with students, but they can't serve all their needs. Although it's a challenge to find the time, we must work together.

Key Point: Engaging Parents as Learning Partners

I never met any parents who didn't want their children to learn and succeed in school. However, because most of my teaching career has been spent in urban settings with large minority populations, or whose parents had minimal education themselves, I've met a lot of parents who didn't know how to help their children learn and succeed in our school system. The self-reported education level of parents in one of the schools where I consult includes only 40 percent who have graduated from high school and 6 percent who have no formal schooling beyond third grade. Nevertheless, all those parents can be teaching and learning partners.

Parent workshops are one way to educate students' parents and engage them as teaching partners. (*Note*: For ease in writing, a parent is any adult outside of the school who serves the student in a supportive role.) At one site a fellow NBCT and I conducted evening workshops for parents in how to look at student work. We began by first introducing the district-mandated content standards that we had converted to user-friendly, non jargon-filled language. For one assignment we worked with the parent participants to develop scoring guides and then scored a class set of assignments from which the names had been deleted. With no exceptions, after a little bit of practice and lots of discussion, the parents graded the student work the same as we had.

Let's use the Say—Mean—Matter strategy to evaluate this activity. (This strategy is discussed in Chapter 4).

> *Say/Do:* Another teacher and I conducted evening workshops to teach parents how to grade their students' schoolwork.

> *Mean:* This meant that parents would be able to go beyond just asking if their children had completed an assignment or not; they would be able to judge the completeness and quality of the students' work.

> *Matter:* This mattered a great deal because it engaged parents as teaching partners and extended the audience for the students' work. It created a partnership between the teacher and the parents. It provided a common communication tool, a scoring guide, for the parent(s) and child to use to gauge the students' work. It opened the teacher's formerly exclusive role in judging the quality of student work by including the parents in this process. The result, for those students whose parents participated, was that their academic achievement rose.

Another technique I've used very effectively, and about which much has been written, is student-led conferencing. I first learned about this strategy when I attended a California Association for Teachers of English (CATE) conference some years ago. Presenting was a group of teachers from a middle school and their students. The students were the stars. They presented their two-year comprehensive portfolios for us to review. Part of their school's graduation requirements included a presentation by each student of an exemplary portfolio. The portfolio consisted of a variety of student work that demonstrated they had met the schools' academic requirements. Before a committee composed of their peers, parents, several teachers, and at least one community member, they defended their work. They had come to the CATE conference to show us what they had done and to tell us how it impacted their middle school experience. The students were articulate, organized, and highly motivated, and they took personal responsibility for the quality and comprehensiveness of the work they had completed. Although I never was able to convince any of the schools where I taught to adopt this graduation requirement, that didn't stop me from implementing it in my own classes.

Four times each school year my students returned to school in the evening, along with one or more of their family members and some refreshments to share. Students, with their families, matched each of the course-related district-mandated content standards to the work they had completed, or were in the process of improving, that represented evidence of accomplishment. The dialogue was between students and their family members. During these evenings my responsibilities were minimal, mostly confined to providing the venue and the structure for the conferences; I was an observer. Where student-led conferences are the norm, student motivation, as well as quality and completeness of work, continues to improve throughout the year. Passing the class is largely based on demonstrated accomplishment, as evidenced in the portfolio, of the content standards for the course. Parents are partners in encouraging and supporting their children.

Just like in the service learning science project outlined earlier, there is an unexpected side effect. Because my students' work was public, that also meant that my assignments to students were public. I couldn't assign anything that didn't help the students to accomplish the content standards at a mastery level. No gimmicky lessons, no accepting poor-quality work. That led to my completely dropping D grades. Student work either met the standard at an accomplished (A), expert (B), or proficient (C) level, or wasn't yet ready for a grade.

Student-led conferences are one way to engage parents; there are also others. One of my very creative fellow teachers used the expertise in her parent community to teach math and social studies/history. Her lessons were embedded in the cultural similarities and differences of her student population. She learned through querying her students about their parents' favorite recipes. She then invited parents to cook for the class. They were thrilled to be asked. The students wrote down the recipes and instructions the parents gave orally. They calculated fractions, checked on the nutritional value of ingredients, and compared similar dishes across cultures and even by country and town of origin within a large cultural group. The parents were empowered; they had something they could teach the teachers and their own children. Feeling valued and welcomed, many parents returned to attend night classes to study English as a new language, to volunteer in the classroom, and to assist with their children's homework. I was reminded, through my colleague, that everyone has value, that everyone benefits by contributing, and that all of us grow stronger within a community of learners.

Key Point: Community Resources

Few teachers develop community partnerships, a subject rarely broached in teacher education programs. Yet many community partnerships exist, waiting to expand. Still more have yet to be cultivated. There is no single model endorsed by the National Board; what follows is again from personal experience.

I am a graduate of the Junior Achievement program. Junior Achievement (JA) is a nonprofit business organization that has been operating in schools for the past nine decades, serving more than two million students in that time. My JA affiliation goes back to my high school years in New York City. A JA group sponsored an after-school program my accounting teacher encouraged us to join. The JA folks taught us to write business plans, develop and sell products, distribute earnings, and do record keeping. What I was learning in my accounting class became real through my JA experiences. I went on to become the NYC JA Treasurer of the Year (1960) and from there attended a national conference, all expenses paid. That was my first trip outside of New York, and still memorable.

Since my high school years JA has expanded into K–12, standards-aligned curriculum. Its programs remain cost-free to schools and students, run by volunteers from the business and local community, and dedicated to introducing students to the free-enterprise system on which our country is based. There's no other political agenda. It primarily serves urban populations but its 123 local offices attempt to reach as many students and teachers as possible. It often waits to be invited into our schools. Junior Achievement is a community-based learning organization that is chartered to work with teachers to improve student learning. Its international members extend the learning opportunities beyond U.S. borders through Internet access. In one of the districts where I consult, it has committed to providing services to 100 classes during this school year. In some parts of the country it has elaborate free enterprise zones that house mock cities. Check for local availability through its web-site: *www.ja.org*.

Key Point: Professional Learning Communities

Professional learning communities are all about continued professional development in collaborative settings. There are many models, informal and formal. J. W. Stigler, a University of California, Los Angeles professor and researcher, popularized one such technique, the Japanese lesson-study model, in his book *The Teaching Gap* (2001). Japanese lesson-study is a technique wherein teachers plan a lesson together, teach it, then analyze the student work that was an outcome of that lesson. They refine the lesson and teach it again. The value is that teachers collaboratively study student work to inform their teaching practice.

There are many other models for teacher collaboration as well. The Critical Friends network, developed through the Annenberg Foundation, is one: *www.criticalfriends.org*. There are less formal ways to collaborate as well. For example, the California Subject Matter Projects, cosponsored by the University of California, encourages professional book groups. Whenever and however teachers get together to analyze student work to inform instruction, to read professional articles or books, or to share lessons, that is a professional learning community. While good teaching can be done in isolation, great teaching thrives on collaboration.

Final Thoughts on the Core Propositions

When I first made the change from corporate executive to classroom teacher I had a teaching credential and knew my content area, but I was otherwise unprepared for my life as a teacher. The isolationism built into most school structures is probably the greatest single factor leading to teacher burnout; it was the one that nearly sent me running from the classroom, save for some amazing colleagues who cared about me, who wanted to help, who offered advice and lesson plans, who even ran interference when I hit the "system." I loved the students and didn't want to leave, but I needed a community of teachers to reach them. Fortunately, I found one.

In my work as an education consultant I seldom encounter teachers who leave the profession because of something the students did or didn't do. Often, they cite working alone and missing meaningful conversations with other adults as their principal reason for leaving education. We need to end the isolation. Teachers are amazing people. They are creative, resourceful, dedicated individuals who are truly committed to making a difference in this world. If alone we can change a student's life, imagine what we could do if we collaborated regularly, if we worked with administrators and district personnel to make the best choices for students, and if we engaged parents and the community as our partners in teaching and learning. Do something good for yourself; take a colleague to lunch, buy two professional books—one to read and one to share, ask an administrator how you can be an instructional leader, engage a parent in looking at their student's work, open your classroom door.

Advocacy

Although this is not a separate core proposition, it very well could be. At no time in our nation's education history has public education been more subject to the political will. Accomplished teachers must take on the role of advocate for our students. We cannot quietly follow the political wind and allow decisions to be made outside of the school setting by people who are neither educators nor researchers in related fields. Too many decisions are being made by textbook publishers and policy makers whose personal agendas do not always feature what is best for students.

We cannot be lone voices, confined to the teachers' cafeteria. Practitioners at every level must be continually vigilant against policies that harm students. We have to learn to use student-generated data, and the latest, most rigorous and relevant research to inform education decisions—within and beyond the classroom. In school districts and in state and federal grant guidelines, we're reading "research based" as the justification for setting policy. Yet when we examine the supporting research, more than 75 percent of it is of very low quality, or paid for by the publisher who will benefit most, or is skewed to support a political agenda that is not in the best interests of our students. Most of us didn't become teachers because we wanted to have a strong political voice, but advocacy for students and public education comes with the territory.

Nuts and Bolts

In order to become a National Board Certified Teacher (NBCT) practitioners must provide *clear, convincing,* and *consistent* evidence they have met the NB standards at an accomplished level. You do this by completing four portfolio entries and taking six 30-minute grade- and content-specific examinations. The four portfolio entries, worth 60 percent of the final score, and the six exams, worth 40 percent of the final score, together comprise the complete assessment.

Score 275 or above and you become a National Board Certified Teacher. If your cumulative score is below 275 the National Board banks your scores and you may retake entries of your choice. (There is more about scores and banking in another chapter.) There are currently twenty-four certificates. It is the intention of the National Board to complete standards and performance assessments for all teachers, be they in the library, on the soccer field, or in the traditional classroom setting. No, the National Board doesn't provide an administrative certificate. That will be up to the administrative associations to develop. Consult the NBPTS website for a list of the currently available certificates and for those in development: *www.nbpts.org/certificates.*

General Portfolio and Assessment Requirements. (Consult Your Certificate for the Exact Requirements)

- Entry 1: Analysis of student work samples. *Note:* WLOE and Music require videos for this entry; art requires a photo storyboard; library media has a collaborative entry. There are additional variations; check your certificate for exact requirements.
- Entry 2: Videotape of a classroom activity featuring students, with accompanying student work.
- Entry 3: Videotape of another classroom activity featuring students, with accompanying student work.

- Entry 4: Documented accomplishments—your personal learning and your professional accomplishments over the past five years, and your outreach with the community and family of your students during your year of candidacy. All activities must contribute to student learning.

Assessment Center:

- Six grade- and content-specific 30-minute examinations. Sample prompts available on the web: *www.nbpts.org/assessments.*

That's it. No surprises, no last-minute changes. Everything upfront before you send any money.

Standards-based Instructional Practice

The National Board uses the best standards-based instructional strategies in the portfolio requirements. At the onset teacher-candidates know the specific standards for each certificate, the scoring guides by which their entries will be assessed, and the complete instructions for each portfolio entry. With some variation, each certificate has the same requirements.

Before you spend any money, you can examine the requirements and determine if you're ready to work towards achieving certification or if you would benefit from filling in some gaps in your practice before attempting certification. The National Board now offers four different cycles during the year in which you can begin your NB certificate. You can select the time period during which you want to complete your portfolio and assessment center exams. It's all up to you. When do you have more available time? What support programs will you participate in and when are they held? When can you arrange for the fee payment? The NBPTS fee is currently $2,300 but expected to rise slightly in the next twenty-four months. You can select a twelve-month window in which to complete your portfolio and take the assessment center exams. This period of time may cover one full school year, or a piece of two school years. You make the choice.

What the NB doesn't tell you, and rightfully so, is which strategies and resources you have to use. There's no script for you to follow. You're the accomplished teacher and you know your students and instructional goals best. If you're asked to select a big idea in science for an Early Childhood entry, it's your call as to which big idea you choose. A sample is provided with the entry instructions. The NB asks in an English Language Arts portfolio entry: *How do your students respond to literature?* But it doesn't tell you which literature to select. You make the choice. You have to explain why you chose the literature (or science experiment, or historical period, etc.) you did; why this literature is appropriate for these students at this time; and then what strategies you used to help students accomplish the instructional goals.

Imagine what teaching might be like, what our students' motivation and accomplishments might look like, if we used similar approaches in our K–12 environments to those the National Board uses with teacher-candidates: standards, clearly written instructions with lots of choice, and scoring guides, provided in advance, by which those standards will be assessed. And lots of opportunities to demonstrate your accomplishment. Completing the National Board portfolio entries provides excellent modeling for converting your class to standards-based instruction.

Getting Started

From the NB website (*www.nbpts.org*), open the standards page and examine the certificate of most interest to you. The certificate you select is dependent on your teaching assignment during the initial year you are working toward certification—not on your college major or credential. For some teaching assignments, several certificates are available. If you are teaching in a bilingual setting, consider English as a New Language as well as your grade-level certificate. If you specialize in art or math, you may elect one of those certificates instead of an elementary generalist certificate. Take the time to check out all the certificates, if more than one is applicable to your teaching assignment. Select the certificate that most closely matches your assignment and your expertise. When in doubt, contact the NBPTS, your support provider, or me (email contacts are answered) and ask for some guidance.

Once you've determined which certificate best fits, go to the portfolio instructions: *www.nbpts.org/candidates/2003_04/portfolio/index.html.* (This website address will change depending on the year of inquiry. When in doubt, start with the NBPTS home page and follow the directions.) Before downloading the whole file, which is upwards of 1MB, go to the overview. The overview appears around page 27 or 28 in most of the certificates. On these pages you'll have an overview of the portfolio entries and the assessment center prompts. This is another opportunity, with minimal investment of time and no financial investment, to consider your current preparedness for this rigorous process. Read through what each entry asks of you. Are you prepared to follow the directions and submit the required materials? Do you have the knowledge to successfully complete the assessment center requirements? If the answer is yes, then it's time to download the standards and instructions—a total of 300-plus pages!

You will need Acrobat Reader to download. The software is available free on Adobe's website, which can be accessed directly from the NBPTS website. Put the standards documents and the instructions in a large binder. You'll be referring to them often throughout the year of candidacy.

Portfolio Instructions

The NBPTS provides an introduction and "getting started" section for each certificate. It takes you back to the standards by which all your submitted work will be assessed. Remember, the portfolio is designed to assess the broadest possible range of your teaching practice. You are encouraged to use student work and videos from several classes if available to you, or you may use one class for all three of the classroom-based entries. Check out these points:

- Each certificate has an age and content parameter in the guidelines. Check these against your teaching assignment.
- On the first page of each entry is a list of the targeted standards for the entry, and an overview. Read the narrative carefully. Highlight the active verbs. Use these verbs in your response.
- Entries 1–3 must come from different units of instruction, different lessons, and different points in time (straight from the portfolio instructions).
- Know the core propositions (they are the big picture) and the specific standards for your certificate; study them, ask yourself what each looks like in your practice.
- There are three types of entries: samples of students' work; videotapes of classroom practice; and documented accomplishments outside the classroom that impact on student learning.
- Protect the anonymity of students and adults, and your school, as instructed. As much as possible do not identify people and places by name; use first names or initials.
- If you put your name on all student handouts and you're submitting some handouts as evidence of your instruction, then remove your name with whiteout. Use only your candidate ID number.
- Follow the instructions. Every entry has page limits for the complete entry. Don't exceed the limits because your extra pages won't get read. There are also suggested page limits for each part of the entry. They are

great guides to how much an accomplished teacher would need to write in order to provide clear, convincing, and consistent evidence of the applicable standards. If your written entry is significantly less than the allowable pages, you probably didn't answer the question very well; reread your response and consider revising.

- Assessors will "see" only what you submit; they won't walk into your classroom to observe. Neither will they call you for clarification.
- Each entry is read by a separate assessor; therefore, it is necessary that some of the information, like the Contextual Information Sheet, be included with each entry, even where you are using the same information for each.
- You need to provide clear, convincing, and consistent evidence that you have met the standards at an accomplished level.

All Entries—Contextual Information

There are two parts to this required sheet. If you teach in only one school, you may only have to complete this sheet once, but you will have to copy it for each entry. Its purpose is to provide the assessor with the big picture of your teaching environment. Because there is no quota for the number of teachers who can be certified each year, there is no advantage or disadvantage if you teach in a rural, suburban, or urban setting. The level of your students' performance is not what is being assessed, it is your teaching and your impact on student learning. Every school and district, each group of students and each individual student, presents a challenge. How well do you know the context of your teaching environment? How does that context impact your teaching choices?

Remember, this is about the big picture; information about the class featured in a specific entry, or about the featured students, will be provided elsewhere.

Student and Adult Release Forms

These forms are mandatory. All students whose work you feature in any entry, or who are seen in any video, must have a release form signed by an adult (if the student is under eighteen). Adults appearing in any video are also required to sign a release form. You do not submit these forms with your entry, but you do sign a statement attesting you have them in your possession. Student and adult release forms come in English and Spanish and are available from the National Board in nineteen different languages. Languages other than English and Spanish may be ordered, without charge, from the National Board: 1-800-22TEACH.

First Three Portfolio Entries—Student Work Samples

In each certificate these entries are based on analysis of student work samples (written, videotape, or pictorial storyboard). In general, each entry asks you to identify the following:

- What are the defining characteristics of the class or student(s) featured in this entry? As you write, consider the purpose and audience. What does the assessor need to know in order to most accurately judge your teaching? What are the challenges this class (this student or these students) present? How does your knowledge of the class/student(s) and their needs at this time affect your choices?
- What are your instructional goals? Why are these goals important for this group of students, at this time? How do these goals build on what the student or students already know? How do these instructional goals move students forward? It's insufficient to say this goal is state- or district-mandated, although that may be part of the equation. You may want to state how the district mandates affect your classroom choices. You still need to make choices and know why you are making the choices you are. What big understandings are worth knowing? How do your choices affect students? I found Grant Wiggins and Jay McTighe's book, *Understanding by Design*, helpful as I thought about essential questions and big understandings.
- How will you know when students achieve the instructional goals? Begin with the end in mind. When you know what student mastery will look like and how it will be assessed, you are in a better position to guide instruction to help students to accomplish the goals. What scoring guide(s) pertain to this assignment, or assignments?
- What do we need to know about the student(s) whose work we are looking at in order to best assess your teaching? Are there defining characteristics of this student's performance? How does it compare to prior performance?

- What instructional strategies did you use to help students to reach the instructional goals? Why did you make those choices?
- What formative (ongoing) and summative (following a lesson or unit) assessments informed your continued instruction?
- What can we learn from analysis of the student-generated work? What did the students learn? What do they still need to learn? What concepts have they mastered? What misconceptions have you addressed or do you still need to address? What can you tell us about what came before and what comes after the lesson featured in this entry (video)?
- What can you learn by analyzing your teaching and the student work generated by this lesson(s)? How can/will you unlearn the things that were not productive? How can you better capitalize on the teachable moments that occurred during this lesson?

Guiding Questions

Each entry features guiding questions. Answer them. They may sometimes seem repetitive, but there are different nuances. For your first draft answer each one as if it were the only question in the entry. When you reread and revise make sure that your response and the accompanying student work (and video, where required) together provide clear, convincing, and consistent evidence of the required standards for this entry.

Computer Templates

Upon beginning each entry it is helpful to create a computer template for the entry. Put your candidate number on the right-hand side of the header. Put the page numbers in the footer. I added the certificate initials and the entry number before my candidate number, just so I wouldn't get confused. It looked like this: EA/ELA #3: 0000000000 (use your candidate number). Type in the guiding questions. Leave space for your answers. Answer each question in order—these are guiding questions. Later on you can delete the questions so your narrative flows more smoothly and you preserve all the available space.

How Your Entry Will Be Scored

In the portfolio instructions for each entry, there is a section "How will my response be scored?" Read it before you start writing. Read it again after you have written your first draft. Then read it still again. Check off each point in your description, analysis, and reflection. Did you provide the evidence the assessor needs to score your entry? Is anything missing? Is your featured lesson/student the best choice to demonstrate your teaching practice for this entry?

SOAPS

SOAPS is a strategy I use with my students when we're studying a piece of literature or writing in any of several genres. Although I'm referring to text (I am an English teacher, after all), you can just as easily use this strategy with film, art, music, and dance. You may find it helpful both in your teaching and as it applies to preparing and then reviewing your portfolio entry.

What Is the Subject?

Students should be able to state the subject, the general topic, content, and ideas contained in the text in a few words or a short phrase. *(You should be able to state the main point of this entry in a few sentences. Just attempting to condense your response will be helpful in clarifying what you want to accomplish with this writing.)*

What Is the Occasion?

It is particularly important that students understand the context the time and place of the piece; the current situation that encouraged the writing to happen. *(This might be a bit of a stretch for you, but think how the bigger context—what was happening in district mandates, in the news, at the school, within your class and with your students, that impacted your choices for this entry. What part of this analysis, if any, would benefit the assessor? How can you weave it into your narrative?)*

Who Is the Audience?

The audience—the group of readers to whom this piece is directed—may be one person, a small group, or a large group. This is a difficult concept for students. They tend to think that authors just write, not that they write for anyone. *(The candidates I assist often have trouble with this idea also. Keep in mind as you write that the assessors are either classroom teachers in your discipline or teachers at your grade level. There are things that are general knowledge, that everyone in the profession knows. You don't have to explain these. There are acronyms peculiar to your locale that do need to be defined; however, they can be defined briefly. You are writing for an educated populace and that gives you some flexibility.)*

What Is the Purpose?

The reason behind the text. Many students do not even consider this question. Until they do, they will not be able to examine the argument or its logic. *(Why are you doing this? What do you hope to demonstrate through this entry? How are you providing evidence for having met the standards at an accomplished level? The answers you come up with won't be included in your written entry, but they will inform and expand your thinking. It's an exercise worth doing.)*

Who Is the Speaker?

When students approach a piece of fiction, they often believe that the author and the speaker of the piece are the same. They fail to realize that in fiction the author may choose to tell the story from any number of different points of view. This is the voice that tells the story. The method of narration and the character of the speaker may be crucial to an understanding of the work.

This confusion of author and speaker is particularly common when there is a gender difference. For instance, students see that the author is female and assume that the speaker is female, even though all the facts indicate that the speaker is male. Furthermore, they think that what the speaker believes is what the author believes. This misconception creates problems for students as they try to unravel meaning. *(Don't lose your voice. This is not an academic, third-party piece of writing. This portfolio is about the work that you do; it's about your students, their lives, what is important in their learning and growth. Don't take a hands-off, academic approach.)*

By using SOAPS as the basis for their analysis, students will discover that a poem or story, historical narrative or other text is carefully structured, creating parameters within which students must work in order to determine meaning. Certainly there is room for different viewpoints because each student brings a unique perspective to the piece. But their conclusions must be supported by the details of the text just as you must provide evidence for all that you claim.

Entry 4—Documented Accomplishments

For all the certificates, the instructions say: "Describe and document those activities associated with your teaching that involve students' families and community [during the current school year], collaboration with colleagues [over the past four years and including the current school year], and your growth as a learner [over the past four years and including the current school year], and that positively impact student learning.

I recommend that you begin with this entry, immediately. As soon as you consider National Board Certification you can begin documenting those activities, formal and informal, you have participated in during the past four years, and those activities you expect to accomplish or are in the midst of completing for the current school year. For some reason, candidates universally struggle with this entry. They are used to thinking about their classrooms and their students, but not as used to thinking about what is going on beyond their classroom. Or they can describe the activities they were involved in, but they can't make the connection between the activity and student learning. Sometimes you have to take time to think it through; sometimes the activity didn't lead to improved student learning. This entry is most closely related to core proposition 5: Teachers are members of learning communities.

Let's start with some general guidelines for entry 4. The assessors are interested in knowing that you are a lifelong learner, that you continue to participate in activities that support your continued professional growth. You work with your colleagues to strengthen one another's practices and contribute to your students' development. You have done both of these on a continuing basis, over the past four years and during this current year. You invite your students' families and the school community to participate as partners in teaching and learning. How you will choose to demonstrate each of these accomplishments and whether your participation is formal or informal are entirely up to you. Each activity featured in this entry must have the following information:

- What did you do? What was the nature of the activity? Keep this description brief. What does the assessor need to know? How much detail do you have to include; what can you leave out? Here's an example from my practice: (Description, or What?) *Every ten weeks students and their families meet at school in the evening to examine the work the students have accomplished since the beginning of the semester and which they have organized into portfolios. We hold these student-led conferences in the school cafeteria because there are usually two hundred or more students and their family members each evening.*

- Why is this activity significant? (This is analysis. It answers the So what? or the What does it mean? part of the entry.) My response: *Student-led conferences are significant because it is often the only opportunity the students and their families have to come together for meaningful conversation about the student's accomplishments and how the student is progressing. It's not about competitive grades, it's about all students taking responsibility for their own learning and for engaging their families as partners in that learning. For a long time I was the only teacher at my school who did student-led conferences; maybe because this was unpaid time. I hold the meetings in the evenings as that is most convenient for the families and attendance is greatest. I know the parents are appreciative because over the last five years I have been conducting student-led conferences, they have been asking their children's other teachers to also have student-led conference nights. One family gave me a copy of the film* Mr. Holland's Opus *because they said I was their student's Mr. Holland.* (*Note:* Even though this activity is supposed to be about what I'm doing this year with the families, I was able to let the assessor know that I've been doing this for a long time. It can't hurt, even if it may not specifically help.)

- How does this activity impact student learning? (Here's the Then what? or the What does it matter? part of the activity and one that poses the most significant challenges for candidates.) How does your activity (and teachers are often in a frenzy of activity) impact student learning? My response continues: *Student-led conferences have had a major impact on my teaching and on my students' learning. They do work knowing their families will see it. They know that they cannot hide behind a missing mark in the roll book when their parent asks about their accomplishment. The audience is bigger and much more important than just the teacher. Students report how proud they are of their work, how much better it is than before, how their families hang their completed work in the house. I wish that this process helped every student to achieve at high levels; sadly it doesn't. While it moves many students along, some still choose not to work, or to take advantage of the many opportunities the school and I make available to them to reach the instructional goals. Since I have instituted student-led conferences, I don't have any parent complaints, nor do students complain about their grades. They know they receive the grades they earn, as shown in the evidence in their portfolios. Grades in general are up, as are my students' standardized test scores.*

Your entries may be longer or shorter depending on the activity you're describing. It is not the number of activities you document for this entry, it's the nature and impact of the activities on student learning. To begin, write up all the activities in which you are or have been engaged. When you've done your first draft you can eliminate those that didn't have a great impact or that can be folded into another activity description. The assessor wants to see clear, convincing, and consistent evidence you have met the targeted standards at an accomplished level. You don't have to try to dump everything you've ever done, just pick the activities that have had the greatest impact on student learning.

Your activities can be formal or informal. Participating in a professional book club can inform your practice more than a course from the university. What is important is that you can make strong connections between the activity and the impact on student learning. You can impact your own students or students of other teachers.

Instructions

For each of the portfolio entries, read the instructions. Use active reading strategies. Each year the instructions are more and more clear in the National Board's attempt to answer the most frequently asked questions. When in doubt, email the National Board and ask for clarification. Nothing you are asked to do is for naught. Everything you do for the portfolio and for the assessment center exams can positively impact your practice and your students.

The Assessment Center

Each candidate will have to respond to six 30-minute exams, completed on the same day unless special accommodations have been made in advance. Sample prompts for each certificate are available on the website. It's a good idea to read through the prompts in advance (they change every year) and determine in advance if you have any gaps in your content knowledge or pedagogy. If so, take the time to learn what you need to be successful. You may only need to brush up, something you can do while you are completing the rest of the portfolio entries. You may realize that there are major holes in your content knowledge; take the time to fill in those holes.

Practical Matters

I recommend that you plan to take your assessment center exams after you have submitted your portfolio. First, you will have spent many months thinking and writing about your teaching; that's great practice for completing the assessment center exams in the limited time available. There's also a practical side. Once you have paid the $2,300 fee to the NB you may withdraw at any time up until you either submit the portfolio or you take the exams. Official withdrawal results in a $2,000 refund. Once you've either taken the tests or submitted your portfolio for scoring, the monies are forfeited, even if you don't complete the rest of the NB process. Since some candidates, in spite of good intentions, don't complete the portfolio, it's in your best interest (just in case) to complete the portfolio before taking the exams.

The National Board offers four different cycles during which you can complete the NB process. Consult the website for details. Select the cycle that best fits into your teaching assignment and works well within the time frame of your other commitments. Your cycle begins when you pay the initial $300. Because the bulk of the materials, the standards, and the portfolio instructions are available to download prior to paying any fees to the National Board, you are encouraged to begin the process before making the financial commitment.

All these options and supports are available for you; use them. This entire process is about your continued professional growth. Take the time you need to get the most out of the experience. The National Board is not going away; it will be here next year and the year after that, and beyond that as well.

How Scoring and Certification Work

There are absolutely no tricks to the scoring. Assessors are well trained. They are encouraged to assume each entry begins with a "3" on a 4-point scale. They will search out evidence of the standard wherever it occurs. Your job is to make it easy by writing clearly and logically, by responding completely to the guiding questions, and by following the instructions. Don't exceed the page limits or the videotape specifications. Assessors will not read beyond the stated number of pages. They won't watch a video beyond the maximum number of minutes. Nor will they examine artifacts that exceed the maximum number of allowable pages—no matter how dynamic and compelling your artifacts are. There are no exceptions.

Each performance is scored independently on a 0.75 to 4.25 Score Scale. The following information is adopted from the National Board scoring guide for assessors.

The Score Scale			
0.75 1.00 1.25	1.75 2.00 2.25	2.75 3.00 3.25	3.75 4.00 4.25
The "1" Family	The "2" Family	The "3" Family	The "4" Family

Candidate performances are assigned a whole number score (1, 2, 3, or 4) and then, if appropriate, the whole number score is augmented with a plus or minus. Plus and minus scores are represented numerically as an increment or decrement of 0.25 from the whole number score. For example, a 1+ is equivalent to a 1.25, a 3– is equivalent to a 2.75. Thus, scores can range from 0.75 to 4.25. Assessors classify performances and put them into the score category that best fits the performance. They may "shade" the score up or down to reflect a strong or weak performance in that family. Families are distinct from one another; cases must ultimately be assigned to one family or another, not in between.

Excellent Teaching Takes on Many Faces

There is no one style or context of teaching that signals a particular point on the score scale. On the contrary, the surface features of teaching are, taken alone, not indicators that determine a teacher's evaluation by NBPTS standards. Assessors are always looking for clear, convincing, and consistent evidence for each of the targeted standards. They are encouraged to assume everyone is a "3" and to look for positive evidence before they note negative evidence.

It helps to think of the scoring scale as a rubric you can divide into two levels. Levels 4 and 3 are both "accomplished" levels. Levels 2 and 1 are both "not accomplished" levels. The assessor looks for key indicators of level of performance.

Here's another way to think of the 4-point scoring scale: 4 = Outrageously Good; 3 = Pretty Darn Good; 2 = Mediocre Overall (may occasionally hint at accomplishment); and 1 = Quite Weak (downright awful). I include this colloquial rubric with a bit of trepidation. If you should score a 1 on an entry, it may very well be that it's not your teaching or the lesson that's downright awful, but the writing about the lesson and student work. When I read entries by candidates who are banking their scores, I often find great gaps between what I see in their classrooms and the evidence they have presented in their portfolio entries. Usually, their teaching practice is better than their writing. Very occasionally, I find a portfolio entry that reads well, but is unsubstantiated by the student evidence.

It is important that you realize that all the assessors will know about your teaching practice is what they read in your entry, see on your video, and find in the artifacts you submit—nothing else. I can't stress this enough.

This past year I read an entry for a candidate who has an outstanding local reputation as an educator. She is often called upon to lead workshops and to mentor new teachers, yet her scores were in the 2 and below range. I was really surprised by what I found in her entries. She had consistently low-level expectations for her students and lots of domesticating strategies, similar to what Patrick Finn writes about in *Literacy With an Attitude*. Working together around her instructional goals, the strategies she used with her students, and what we found in her student work opened the dialogue about her teaching. She was surprisingly willing to share, to grow, and even to unlearn some of the teaching practices she had come to rely on.

It's easy to believe your own press, to fall into a complacent mode and avoid challenging yourself and your students. In many districts (and sadly common in urban centers like the one where I work), expectations for

The Teacher's Guide to National Board Certification

teachers and students are low. It is often not until teachers challenge their practice against the high National Board standards that one sees the discrepancies. If everyone around you is doing level 2 teaching, how would you know there's more to be accomplished?

Unevenness Across the Score Levels

The National Board uses the term "uneven" in the rubric to describe one way a 3 differs from a 4, but cases at all levels of performance can show unevenness. In a 3 some parts of the performance may be exceptionally good, and some only okay, but overall, the performance indicates accomplishment. Or, a 3 may be quite steadily accomplished, but not exceptional. A 2 may also be uneven, but some 2s only hint at accomplishment, rising occasionally to a low 3 level. Twos may also be quite steadily mediocre. Ones are generally weak, though some 1s may show a hint of 2-ness.

In the many hundreds of entries I have read, in a variety of certificate areas, where candidates provide clear, consistent, and convincing evidence of having met the targeted standards, the scores are high.

Writing Ability and Organization

I'm going to really veer from the National Board rhetoric on this one. I think, and have seen in a couple of hundred entries, that writing does count. It's not about style, but it is about clarity, the conventions of standard written English, and organization that allows assessors to readily find the evidence that you are documenting. That said, I don't recommend that you hire a ghost writer to rewrite what you've done. Instead, challenge yourself and have other candidates read your entry and ask the tough questions (in a kind and supportive way). While you aren't expected to be a Hemingway, you should strive to write in a clear, straightforward manner.

Assessors are instructed to look for evidence wherever they find it in the response. For ease of writing and revision, try to respond to the guiding questions sequentially. Assessors won't officially take points off for disorganization, but they're just human. If they have to hunt, they may not hunt for the evidence as diligently as you have obscured it, although they will attempt to find every bit of evidence that taken together satisfies the standard.

Halos and Sudden Death

When I attended the scoring institute in Washington, D.C., I was intrigued by these two ideas. The first, the halo effect, occurs when something the teacher does is so singularly impressive that the assessor loses sight of the rest of the performance. I thought about the times I've been fooled by beautiful bulletin boards only to discover, upon more careful examination, that there was no substantive student work displayed. Or when the reputation of the popular teacher shielded the real lack of content in the lessons.

The pitchfork, or sudden death, effect, is the opposite of a halo effect. This occurs when a teacher commits an error or blunders something in a way that so completely offends the assessor that he or she fails to see what is good in the response. One of the videos I viewed, as a support provider, not as an assessor, left me completely underwhelmed by the teacher's slovenly dress. Although I still don't approve of the unprofessional dress I find at many schools, it should rightfully not be the prime determiner of a teacher's effectiveness. When I viewed the video in question a second time, I was able to get past the appearance and really watch and listen to the exchanges between the teacher and the students. There were high-order thinking questions with lots of discussion between teacher and students and between the students. I still have to swallow my initial reaction and suggest to the teacher candidates I support that they avoid any potential problems in advance. If you're not sure what they may be, ask your colleagues to read an entry or view a video. Anything that stands in the way of getting to the essence of the entry is probably better to avoid.

Final words about scoring

I'd make absolutely certain that I followed the instructions for page limits, font style and size, and page margins. I wouldn't want anyone to be "thrown out" based on a technicality. In order for the National Board to be fair to all candidates, and to provide an equal opportunity to achieve for everyone who completes the process, it is necessary to adhere to the same format standards for everyone. Follow the instructions.

A final, final word: Leave the flash at home. No color printers, no fancy type setting, no printing front and back. Just follow the instructions and get the job done.

The Teacher's Guide to National Board Certification

Time Management

In my work with teacher-candidates there are two factors that most often lead to noncertification. The first of these is the candidate's writing ability. The second is poor time management and the unproductive worrying that seems to accompany it. What follows are the words, reprinted with permission, from a 2001–2002 candidate. Her experience is what we want to avoid, the last-minute crunch.

> I spent the last 5 days at the computer writing for 8–11 hours. The day before that, I spent rereading portions of my second language acquisition books and making notes on index cards. That was a valuable tool for entry 1. My living room where my desk is, looks awful. There are papers, books everywhere. Even my cat thinks it is embarrassing. Tomorrow, I will put whatever I have in THE BOX. Then I will pick up the mess in my apartment and reward myself by going for a long walk. I have not been outside at all for 6 days. I once fed my son a dinner of ice cream and tapioca pudding because I felt I had no time to cook. I feel ashamed. I think that the support groups should offer advice on how to manage stress while we work on NB. It would help expert worriers like me. I sometimes consider worrying my favorite indoor sport.

The best cure for procrastination is good planning right from the onset. Even if you're not a procrastinator, completing the NB requirements takes many months, plenty of time for the unexpected to occur. By starting early and doing some long-term planning, you can avoid many of the pitfalls other candidates have experienced—including having to drop out because their portfolios weren't ready on time.

Before you even begin the NB process take the time to examine your current commitments. What activities currently fill each 24-hour day? Don't forget to include things like sleeping and eating, personal relationships, teaching, volunteer activities, after-school meetings, children's needs, grading papers, attending Open House and committee meetings, your favorite TV show, religious life, and yoga practice. Include every activity that you currently engage in.

I've never met a teacher who had free time at the end of each day, so it's most likely that in order to find time for the National Board process you'll have to figure out what activities you can condense or eliminate. This is a great opportunity to set some priorities for what is really important. Personally, I put cleaning house way at the bottom of the list and yoga classes towards the top. Donald Graves suggests you dump those people or activities that take energy away from you and increase your contact time with the people and events that give you energy. Whatever criteria you choose, figuring out where the time will come from is an important initial step.

The NB process will most likely require one structured three-hour meeting each month. (I'm basing this on the typical candidate support program. If yours is different, adjust accordingly.) In addition, plan on one cohort meeting each week. Two and a half to three hours seems to be the ideal length for a productive meeting. Again, adjust based on your own experience. In addition to meeting with others, you'll need to set some time aside each week to analyze student work, to rewatch your videos, to reflect on your teaching and learning, and to write and revise your portfolio entries. This time has to come from somewhere. The question for you to answer is where is the time going to come from?

As you're deciding how you'll manage time for this new commitment, talk to your significant others, spouse and children in particular. Make the case why achieving National Board Certification will benefit the family (perhaps financial incentives, opportunities for advancement, prestige, and personal satisfaction). What support will your family be able to provide? What tasks can they do that you do now? Have a similar conversation with your site administrator. Are there committees you can set aside this year? Assure her that she is not losing a dedicated teacher forever; you'll be even more energized next year. Since schools, like most organizations, follow the rule of 20 (20 percent of the people do 80 percent of the work) administrators tend to rely on the same 20 percent of the faculty to do all the extra jobs. Losing one of them can negatively impact the school site. On the other hand, you need and deserve time for personal professional development. Make your case compassionately, be flexible where you can, then stick to what you believe is the right action for you at this time. A good question to ask an adamant administrator, or a less than supportive significant other, is: "What would you like me to set aside so I can do the activity you want me to do?"

Choices

Thanks to the increasing number of applicants, the National Board now offers four cycles each year from which you can select the time frame that best suits your schedule. Remember that the cycle you're in is determined

The Teacher's Guide to National Board Certification

by when you submit your application and the required $300 application fee. From the time you submit, you'll have eight to twelve months to complete the portfolio and the assessment center. You don't have to wait until you submit your fees in order to begin the NB process. Gather information, resources, and colleagues. Reread the Nuts and Bolts chapter. Once you have your resources in place you can submit the application.

National Board Certification is a voluntary process. The best time to attempt certification is when you're ready.

Candidate Cohorts—Lean on Me

I could not have completed the National Board requirements successfully had I not had colleagues sharing the process with me. When we began the NB portfolios in the spring of 1997, there were no support groups in our area. I began the first one at UCLA, corralling seventeen other teachers to take the journey with me. They were wonderful and as essential to my success as I was to theirs. In the five-plus years that I have been supporting candidates, it is always the cohort groups the candidates form that impact their NB process even more than the support and guidance I provide.

I strongly recommend that you join with a few colleagues to undertake this professional journey together. In the support groups I've conducted in southern California I always encourage candidates to participate in a formal support network and to link up with a few other candidates as well. This is becoming easier as more teachers are challenging themselves and undertaking the NB process.

It is not enough, however, to just get together with colleagues and work on the portfolio entries; there's some learning that needs to happen first—at least it did for me. Placing teachers together in a group doesn't guarantee they will work well together, or that they will even know how to work together around the NB process. Group work takes focus, practice, and good intentions. Successful cohort groups are formed based on some of these characteristics:

- Candidates work at the same school site, teach the same grade level or discipline, or are working on the same certificate.
- Cohort members are the only teacher-candidates in the area—these teachers are often the first in their district, the risk takers who set the standard.
- Members have a similar work ethic—it's unduly stressful when one member thinks a scheduled meeting is firm and another takes it as a loose target to shoot for.
- Everyone presumes others have good intentions—no flying off the handle over a misconstrued comment. The assumption is that all are interested in improving student learning and successfully completing NB certification.

- There's a strong commitment to working together until the portfolios are completed and submitted—even if a member withdraws from the NB process. No one quits on the group. If you do withdraw, you remain as a coach this year and know you'll get coached the following year.
- Candidates find a common meeting time and place that's agreeable to everyone. Public places, such as restaurants, generally don't work well—too many distractions. Meeting after school or in one another's homes is often the best solution. Set meeting dates and times far in advance and then don't change, except for truly unavoidable life emergencies.
- The group establishes rules that work for the members—keep them simple.
- Don't make food the center of attention during the meetings. Although snacks help to create a relaxing atmosphere and nourish the body, worrying about what to prepare may not. Keep the refreshments simple.
- Everyone maintains a sense of humor.
- The focus is on student achievement, great teaching, and certification.

Safe and Productive Learning Environments

Once you've chosen your group, how do you proceed? For most candidates, sharing their students' work and their own teaching practices is a new phenomenon and may cause some initial tension. Add to that exposing your writing about your practice to others, in a high-stakes environment, and the level of stress can soar. You want the process and the time you spend meeting and examining your entries to be productive, not destructive. That means that just as we need to establish safe learning environments for our students, we need safe professional learning environments as well. It's a good idea for the group to do a collective reading of the NB teaching standards that pertain to learning environment and discuss how the key points relate to the group.

The Meeting

You've met, you've established your group norms, and you've calendared dates and times to meet. You've agreed that you may need to add meetings as you approach the portfolio due date or the assessment center exams. Everyone comes to the meeting on time and prepared. It's frustrating when you come to the meeting prepared and no one else is ready to share their work, or they haven't done anything yet and instead of collaborating, you're in the scolding or pleading mode, or worse, you leave in disgust. One way to avoid this pitfall is at the end of each session determine what should be accomplished in preparation for the next meeting. For example, you may collectively assign completing the student release forms, doing the first practice video, gathering artifacts for entry 4—documented accomplishments, writing a draft of an entry, bringing student work to analyze together, sharing a lesson you're thinking of featuring. Don't be surprised if teachers you thought you knew, and whom you've chosen to work with because you have so much in common, turn out to have very different work styles. Different work styles doesn't necessarily mean that one is better than another, but if one is always prompt and another is a procrastinator, there's going to be wasted time, bad feelings, and more stress.

Reflect and negotiate. Take time out to write down your learning and working styles. What characteristics in another can you live with? Which are simply unacceptable? You will be spending about eight months with your cohort group members; you want the time to be as productive as possible. You don't want to leave each session more stressed than when you began. Cohort groups should be about support and learning.

Next time you assign students to work together in a group on a long-term project, think about your group experiences and what you learned that you might share with your students. Encourage them to reflect on successful and unsuccessful groups they've worked with and how they can be more productive in the future. Collaboration is an integral part of most work environments. Spending time learning how to do it well is valuable, for yourself and for your students.

Looking at Student Work Protocols

A protocol is an agreed-upon procedure for doing something. In this case, the protocol is for looking at student work, or at a candidate's work. Instead of taking time here to describe the many different protocols available that you can follow as written or use to design your own, I'm going to direct you to a wonderful website: *www.lasw.org*. From this website you can investigate some of the protocols frequently used to examine student work. They are offered as models, to follow exactly or to work from. I usually find that when we begin by requiring cohorts to follow the protocol for the first couple of times they examine student work, or one another's work, they soon develop their own rhythm and way of doing things. Eventually they set the protocol aside and work collaboratively without one.

With or without a fixed protocol, when you meet as a group determine how long the meeting will last, then divide the time by the number of candidates who brought the agreed-upon assignment to share. Don't let anyone hog the meeting. Use whatever means necessary to provide time so everyone has an equal opportunity to get their work read and commented upon. I find a kitchen timer works well and removes the onus from any one person having to be the timekeeper.

Reflective Conversation Questions

You might consider using some form of the reflective conversation questions that follow to guide the group discussion. As you become more comfortable working together you'll have less and less need to rely on these somewhat artificial sentence starters, but they do help in the beginning. There are three basic types of reflective conversation questions: paraphrasing, clarifying, and mediational.

Paraphrasing

Paraphrasing is a restatement of the speaker's comments put into the listener's words. Paraphrasing is important in assuring that everyone hears the same thing and has the same understanding. Frequently the speaker, upon hearing the paraphrase, restates or clarifies and corrects. Paraphrasing shows the speaker that you are actively listening. Paraphrases often draw out additional comments. These are sentence starters:

- In other words . . .
- What I'm hearing then . . .
- What I hear you saying . . .
- From what I hear you say . . .
- I'm hearing many things . . .
- As I listen to you I'm hearing . . .

Clarifying

Clarifying seeks understanding by avoiding misunderstanding. Clarifying asks for additional information by requesting the speaker to fill in the gaps. This is very important as it is common to leave large holes in our explanations when we are close to a subject, when we know it very well or have worked with it for a long time. The work becomes obvious to us, while it may remain unclear to the rest of the group. When our group members ask for clarification, we should listen to their comments. If they are not finding the information or explanation they need for complete understanding, there's a strong possibility the assessors won't either.

- Would you tell me a little more about . . .
- Let me see if I understand . . .
- It'd help me understand if you'd give me an example of . . .
- So, are you saying/suggesting . . .?
- Tell me what you mean when you . . .
- Tell me how that idea is like (different from) . . .
- To what extent. . .?
- I'm intrigued by . . .

Mediational

Mediational questions are a bit more challenging. The listener hears, or sees on a video, or reads in a candidate's entry something that indicates a wrong turn. These questions push the speakers to reexamine their thinking, or their lesson. They suggest, without saying outright, that there may be a better way of reaching the instructional goal, or another explanation for the student outcomes. Use these carefully. Candidates should assume group members all have good intentions and are not being unduly critical.

- What's another way you might . . .?
- What would it look like if . . .?
- What do you think would happen if . . .?
- How was . . . different from (like) . . .?
- What's another way you might . . .?
- What sort of an impact do you think . . .?
- What criteria do you use to . . . ?
- What do you think . . .?
- How did you decide (come to that conclusion) . . .?
- What might you see happening in your classroom if . . .?

Ultimately, each candidate decides for themselves what to include or exclude from an entry. The role of the group is to guide, poke, prod, support, and encourage.

Another way to examine member's entries is by asking similar questions to those the assessors are instructed to ask themselves during scoring:

- Are the goals of the lesson worthwhile and appropriate, even if they are not goals that you would choose for your students?
- Is the candidate demonstrating knowledge of students as individuals or as a developmental or social group, even if the approach is different from one you would take?
- Is the candidate showing command of the content and making connections, even if they are not the connections you would make?
- Are students engaged in the lesson, even if it's not in a way you are used to?
- Is the candidate showing respect for all students, even if the candidate's style is different from yours?
- Is there something troubling you about the candidate's choice of content, style, classroom organization, or presentation of material? Ask for clarification, without challenging, of why these choices were made. Refer to the mediational questions above.
- What is the underlying structure of this performance? What is going on beneath the surface features? For example, what is the level of resources in the classroom? How are you affected by the teacher's and students' accents and appearance? What about the noise level? Is the candidate's writing ability, as demonstrated in the response, getting in the way of an accurate assessment?

Scoring One Another's Entries

My best advice to you is, don't. You wouldn't want to be in the position of telling your colleague that this is a great entry, a definite 3+, only to have the entry receive a lower score. Instead, help one another to document clear, convincing, and consistent evidence of the targeted standards in each entry. Here's how:

- Begin with a three-column blank sheet. On the left-hand column list the key points for each of the targeted standards for this entry. This is a great way to review the standards.

- In the center column jot down a key word or phrase each time you find evidence of the key point in the standard. Seek evidence wherever you find it. Evidence will not be in the same order as the key points you've listed. Search for evidence throughout the entry.
- The candidate reviews your notes and the comments of other cohort members who have read the candidate's response to this portfolio entry. The candidate determines whether or not he or she has provided clear, convincing, and consistent evidence of the targeted standards. Cohort groups are stating the facts, nothing but the facts, as they find them. They are not taking on the responsibility for scoring the entry. That is rightfully the sole responsibility of the candidate. Trust me on this one.

The Affective Domain

Cohort groups do the work with you. They examine your entries, check your grammar and format, and provide lots of other important assistance. They are also the colleagues who will spur you on when you're thinking of quitting. They're the teachers who will help you see through a piece of student work and make sense of it when you can't. They'll encourage you, applaud your efforts, commiserate when factors beyond your control get in the way of your progress. They are also the colleagues who, in the best of working relationships, will be honest about what they read in your entries and see in your videos. They are critically important. They will support you in ways the official support provider (and that's assuming you're fortunate enough to have an experienced, highly knowledgeable support organization in your geographic area) cannot. You'll bond with these colleagues and come to rely on them to discuss your practice and the challenges your students present. Even after you've achieved certification, they will continue to encourage you to grow as a professional. If you are unfortunate enough to be in an environment where high standards are not the norm, for students or teachers, it's extremely helpful to be with a group that respects high standards and high expectations for everyone in the learning community. If you take no other advice from this book, take this. Leave teacher isolation behind—permanently.

A Cautionary Word

Here's a cautionary word I wish I didn't have to add. The widespread recognition of National Board Certification as an integral part of the professional continuum may be our best opportunity to gain the respect we deserve as a profession. It is critically important, therefore, that no black marks are associated with this process or with the teachers who achieve certification. Occasionally I will be called upon by a principal to check on an NBCT whom they think has low standards. I do this unofficially; I'm not an investigator for the National Board. Very rarely, after observing the teacher in question, do I agree with the principal's assessment, but occasionally I do. Then I wonder how the teacher became certified. I'm sure that it is possible, although not likely, that a teacher can make a great written case and present their practice in a way that demonstrates having met the standards. Recently, I worked with a teacher-candidate about whom I had strong negative feelings—which I kept to myself until she showed her hand. She engaged in some blatant copying. She described as her documented accomplishments the work of two other candidates from her cohort group. She wrote up a lesson someone else had done and shared with the cohort, presenting it as her original idea. Everyone was appalled, but no one knew how to confront this candidate, who was well known in her school for having a violent temper.

The National Board encourages collaboration, not cheating. I advise my candidates to state in their entry when the lesson is the result of collaboration or a formal team effort. It's critical, however, that whatever student work you present was the result of your teaching efforts, not someone else's. Because I had firsthand information about the candidate's accomplishments, I forwarded her name and ID number to the assessment division of the National Board. They investigate by comparing submitted entries. Although I do not attempt to be judge or jury in these cases, and there have been a few others as well, I make it very clear to the candidates I support that I will report any suspected cheating. I hope that all candidates feel the same way. If we wish to be treated as professionals, if we want NB certification to continue to be a recognized distinction worth achieving, then we need to hold ourselves to very high standards, without exception.

Videotaping

Each certificate requires two or three videotaped sequences featuring students and the teacher. The National Board has done an excellent job of providing thorough videotaping instructions. Consult the portfolio instructions *Tips for Videotaping*. I'm not going to repeat what you can readily find there. I do, however, want to use these pages to add some additional commentary to issues addressed in the instructions and to make some suggestions about how to use videotaping to improve your classroom practice and student performance.

First, I have to share my first taping experience, which closely resembles the experiences of many of the candidates I have assisted. On first view all I could see was my weight, my hairdo, and the clothes I was wearing. It was all about me. Most candidates feel the same way. Get over it. It's not about your personal appearance, mannerisms, or your accent, at all. Assessors are taught to go way beyond that. It's all about your teaching and your interaction with students. It's about how you engage students, how you encourage participation. It's about those ongoing teachable moments.

Even though the Board suggests you can use a college student or one of your own students to do the videotaping, here are a couple of words of caution. The college students who are studying cinematography all want to be movie directors. They won't understand that you want a thirty-second pan and then want them to hold the camera still. They will tend to zoom in and out, go wide angle and then pan out, focus on a student who's doing something odd. Your students won't be much worse, except they will probably give special screen time to their friends, or to their enemies if they're goofing off. Professional paid videographers are likewise not the best choice. They love special effects, a definite no-no. In my experience, the best person to do your videotaping, and it does help to have another person do it for you, is another NB candidate. They know exactly what the Board wants in a videotape. They're committed to helping you, especially if you're helping them. If possible, make arrangements to videotape one another.

Practice videotapes are a completely different story and can serve a multitude of purposes. The practice videotape I did for the portfolio actually led to my incorporating video on a regular basis into my classroom practice. My first videotaping went fairly smoothly. The equipment functioned well, the student videographer behaved, you could even hear the student voices, although I provided little opportunity for them to speak. I filled most of the video with my own voice! We all think we look and act differently than we look and act on the video; that was certainly true for me. I really had to swallow hard before allowing anyone else to see my practice videos. To this day, no one has seen the first practice video I did. Occasionally, when I'm feeling too much like a know-it-all I take it out and replay it for an audience of one— me. In that tape it was painfully obvious that I talked way too much. In fact, I talked most of the time. The term *motormouth* fits pretty well. Had I been asked to evaluate my teaching prior to the taping experience I would have said that we have great conversations in my class; that students are motivated, that they participate all the time, that I leave no child behind. The tape showed something very different. And I have learned a great deal since then, and improved my practice along the way.

Just as I improved my teaching by analyzing my videos, students can and will do the same thing. Consider having students tape a dry run of presentations they are required to do: scenes from plays, poetry recitals, student-led conferences. Have them analyze their performances; discuss what their strengths were and what they need to improve. Seeing and hearing themselves on video has more impact than your evaluation, and it can move them to improve because they want to, not because you say they must. Students who mumble, who don't look at the audience, or who act inappropriately silly, get a clearer understanding of what they're doing when they observe their own actions. Of course, the classroom environment must be supportive and free from ridicule or the video will become just another way to be mortified. Small groups, even single students, can analyze videos. One student can tape another, or a small group, and the group can then together analyze their findings.

A Cheap Classroom Tool

Videotape is a much underused classroom tool. The cost is now minimal enough that every school can have several machines; teachers benefit from having their own or from sharing with just a few other teachers in close proximity. Think about the power of students taping a lab experiment, then carefully documenting the steps they took as well as their findings.

Use video for classroom management. It's very powerful to tape a class and then play it back, asking the students to watch for their own behavior, to document when they were on or off task, to count how many times they spoke, and to transcribe and analyze what they said. A video can be equally powerful for you to improve your classroom management techniques. Viewing your video with a seating chart in hand, record how you moved about the room, follow your eye movement, note which students you called on the most or not at all. Videotaping and analyzing several tapes helped me to uncover all sorts of inequities in my classroom. I discovered that I am partial to the right side of the room. I even stand with my body slightly turned to the right. If they wanted to avoid work my students quickly learned they should sit on my left. Not anymore, because now I'm very conscious of my natural preferences and I work at being more equitable.

For another taping session I asked a student sitting in the back to hold the camera at his eye level and allow it to go where he wanted, to follow his mind's eye for twenty minutes. That was also an informative tape. I saw my class the way a student does. If this student was typical, and I picked him because I thought he probably was representative of his classmates, students don't spend very much of their time on-task. I continue to work on engaging my audience, be they K–12 students or adult learners.

One last example of how valuable the video has been in my practice. During one year I had a particularly rambunctious class. I couldn't quite figure out why they were such cutups, but I suspected a ring leader and thought I knew who it was. Then the videotape happened and I knew for sure. I set the camera on a tripod off to the side, the way the NB instructions suggest. From that angle you could see most of the class. It wasn't long before the students pretty much forgot it was there and went on about their daily business. I pride myself on being a pretty observant teacher and don't think too much gets by me. After all, I've raised five children and was on high alert for all their teenage years. I thought what's a class full of other people's kids compared to raising my own. I have since discovered from my adult children that a lot more got by me than I knew at the time. Likewise in my class. That evening when I viewed the tape, off to the right—my left—Daniel sat in a group with his friends. They were a high-performing group I often left to their own devices while I worked with struggling learners. What we captured on tape, however, was not this high-performing, task-oriented group, but Daniel the clown. He did everything he could to keep his friends in smirks (They didn't laugh out loud—that would have been a giveaway—but they smirked a lot.) including, at one point, lying full-length across the top of the desks. That did it, I had him. The next day I returned to class with the video and a TV set. I played the section of the tape featuring Daniel. I was stone-faced, enjoying every moment. I told the class that I had similar documentary evidence on several other students, which was a stretch of the truth, and that I would play the tape for their parents if I didn't see a marked change in their behavior. Everyone shaped up. I kept that video camera on the tripod most of the time. That I didn't tape very often, the red light wasn't even on, seemed to matter less than the possibility I would.

I know that was a long way to go to make the suggestion that you use videotaping to inform your practice and to assist students in improving their performance as well. I hope you'll find the suggestions valuable and that you'll use the National Board process as a catalyst to enhance your teaching.

SOAPS Revisited

Let's return for a moment to a review of the SOAPS strategy presented in Chapter 6. Only this time, let's specifically apply SOAPS to videotaping.

- S—What is the *subject* of the tape? What big idea do you want the audience to come away with after viewing your videotape? You should be able to state this in a few words. For example: I want the audience (think assessors) to value the dynamics of the discourse in my class. Or, in this science lesson I want the assessors to appreciate how student-generated questions guide the laboratory experiment.
- O—The *occasion* should be clearly stated in your analysis. What came before the videotaped segment? How did what came before directly lead to what we're seeing in the videotape? Why is this sequence important for these students at this time?
- A—Who is the *audience*? This is an easy one to answer. The ultimate audience for this videotape is the assessor who will be scoring your entry. Are you providing what the assessor is seeking? Does this video follow the instructions? Is the analysis cognizant of the guiding questions? Have you explained everything that is happening in the video? The assessor who scores this entry is also a classroom teacher. You don't need to apologize if one of the students does something that embarrasses you. That's the beauty of having scoring done by our peers, not by an outside agency. Teachers understand, they've been there—they're there right now! You do have to explain what is happening. In the tape I submitted for one of my entries I had to explain why there was so much quiet time. I had worked very hard to allow "wait time," time for students to think before having to respond. The quiet time, I explained, was really thinking time and as such was critical to my students' learning. Don't apologize; do explain what the assessor is seeing.

Students are particularly helpful in this role. My students, and their families, all knew I was working on certification; they cheered me on every step of the way. I brought the videos I planned to submit to class and asked the students to analyze them. They pointed out some of their behaviors I had missed, and some of my own. They taught me things about their thinking and why they had responded as they did. They were amazingly honest. One student told me that he fumbled for paper, a movement captured on the tape, to avoid answering a question, a technique he used often because it worked. I learned so much by listening to them analyze the video, and then I incorporated their insights into my written analysis. It does take a community to raise a child, and the children, our students, should be part of that learning community.

- P—What is the *purpose* of this videotape and analysis? While the main purpose may be to fulfill the portfolio requirements, until you examine the purpose behind the featured lesson or assessment or experiment, your response will address only the surface elements. Take this opportunity to dig more deeply into your teaching and the students' learning. You should be able to explain everything the assessor will see in the video, read in the accompanying analysis, and verify through the students' work artifacts you provide with your entry.
- S—Who is the *speaker*? The speaker is the voice that tells the story. In this case, it's yours. Don't lose your voice. Occasionally I'll read a candidate's entry and think I'm reading an essay submitted for a juried journal. It's full of references to researchers; learning theories are featured and the teacher is lost. Nowhere in the instructions are you asked to include the names of the researchers who inform your practice. That said, if you know them and it is appropriate to include the reference, go ahead. There's no guarantee that the assessor will know who you are referencing, and less that they will care. What is important here is that you use your knowledge to inform your instruction. I'm reminded of the candidate who included lots of quotes, but made the most outrageous statements about his students. It was obvious to me that while he had book knowledge, he hadn't developed understanding and certainly didn't apply what he'd read.

References

There's no average number of references you should aim for. I've read high-scoring entries with no specific references to research that displayed deep knowledge of how students learn. I've read others, like the one mentioned above, that were full of other people's words, none of which appeared to inform the teacher's practice. You decide how best to highlight your own practice. The portfolio is a performance-based assessment of your teaching practice as demonstrated through description, analysis, and reflection featuring videotape of classroom practice and student artifacts. *You* are crucial; don't lose yourself or your students by trying to impress someone with your education jargon.

Classroom Discourse

Some years ago while I was teaching in an urban high school with a high percentage of poor minority students, I was intrigued by the students who were thriving in spite of all the data that indicated they couldn't. These were the students who would continue their education, in spite of being the first in their family to graduate from high school, or rising out of poverty, or coming from dysfunctional families. They didn't just survive in school, they thrived.

As chance would have it, just when I was thinking about these students I happened to attend a workshop on discourse. The speaker used a phrase, Quality Verbal Interaction, to explain the importance of classroom discourse. I put the two ideas together and returned to my classroom. Using a Sunday comic strip about the upcoming presidential election, I asked the students to have a conversation at home about what this comic strip said, what it meant, and why it was important, if indeed it was. I wasn't as interested in their responses as I was in whether or not they would have a conversation at home. Here's what happened.

The next day one of the young women loudly proclaimed that she would never do that assignment again. She said that her "auntie" sat her down and talked to her for nearly three hours. My student learned that her aunt had never missed an opportunity to vote in nearly forty years. She complained about her aunt taking up her entire evening, but she reported proudly. I wasn't surprised that this student was in the top 5 percent of the school. Nor was I surprised by the number of students who came back to tell me that their mother, or brother, or other caregiver said to go away and wouldn't talk at all. I know there was a wide range of reasons for this behavior, some very legitimate, including that it might have just been an off-night. But I've also read the statistics that say that the average parent and child engage in only a few minutes of conversation a week; most of their verbal exchanges are about directions like *pick up your clothes* or *do your homework*. The very unscientific experiment I conducted disclosed a high correlation between my students who reported having conversation at home and their success in school. There was likewise a strong correlation between low school achievement and students who reported minimal at-home discourse. Although teachers may not be able to change at-home discourse, we can strive to provide lots of opportunities for in-school, in-depth conversation.

Patrick Finn identifies the level and content of classroom discourse as distinguishing features of domesticating and liberating, or empowering, education. One way to increase the power of classroom discourse is with Socratic seminars. If you don't already use this technique as one way to analyze text (Again, you can substitute film or art or music for text.), you might want to investigate the possibilities. The Say—Mean—Matter strategy presented elsewhere in this book also pushes students to go beyond the surface features of a text and uncover the deeper context through discourse.

The Art of Questioning

I remember reading somewhere that about 85 percent of classroom conversation consists of the teacher asking questions of the students. Of this 85 percent spent on questioning, most questions teachers ask fall into the "known-response" category. Known-response means the teacher already knows the answer and the student knows the teacher knows. Students refer to this kind of questioning as "guessing what's on the teacher's mind." Some kids are better at it than others. If you want to get a true picture of the discourse in your classroom and of the types of questions you ask, take the time to transcribe one of your classroom videos. Transcription is a time-consuming but very valuable experience. Although I know some teachers have paid or persuaded others to transcribe for them, it's worth doing yourself. You'll learn a lot more about what is happening in your classroom when you read and listen to yourself and to your students.

Questions generally fall into three categories. Strong students, and these aren't defined by only those who earn good grades, continually ask questions. Questioning is an important strategy for reading and learning in general; it can be explicitly taught and practiced. Teachers can model the art of questioning.

Level 1 questions can be answered explicitly by facts contained in the text or by information accessible in other resources. These test for recall and comprise most of the questions we ask in class. Teachers usually wait an average of less than three seconds between the time they ask a student a question and the time they expect an answer. When students hesitate, or otherwise remain silent, teachers generally move on to another student, or answer the question themselves. Students know this. After seeing my own behavior in one of my early videos I trained myself to wait up to three full minutes before moving on. What I uncovered were the voices and responses of students who usually don't respond at all. They needed the extra time to think, to retrieve the requested information. Here's another *trust me:* as awkward as you'll feel waiting for up to three minutes in a silent classroom, the students will feel even more awkward. Eventually someone will speak out; these responses are usually more thoughtful than the quickly blurted-out answer. For those students who always have their hands up, I ask them to remain quiet for a few moments, to think of a more comprehensive response while allowing another student to answer this time. It's a delicate balance between calling on those who know the answer quickly and allowing time for all students to think. Waiting provides a more equal opportunity to learn for students who are more thoughtful than they are quick.

Level 2 questions have answers that are implied in the text. They require analysis and interpretation of specific parts of the text. They are more challenging because they are open-ended, but we can generally, although not always, come to some consensus around the answers.

Level 3 questions are open-ended and go beyond the text. They are intended to provoke a discussion about an abstract idea or issue that may have been raised in the text or picture or object. They usually don't have a specific answer and may not have any answer at all. These are the essential questions that Grant Wiggins and Jay McTighe identify (Wiggins, 1998).

Essential Questions

Wiggins and McTighe write about asking the essential questions and using these questions to drive curriculum. In order to do this we first have to think about what is worth knowing and what is worth understanding.

There isn't room to discuss their complete design in this context, but I would like to leave you with one example of how high-level questioning can lead to quality verbal interaction.

I have given a lot of workshops on literacy, specifically content-area literacy for secondary students. One of the techniques I employ is the KWL (see Chapter 2) to investigate what students already know. This technique solicits what the students already *know* about a topic; then it generates a list of things they *want* to know; finally, it investigates what they *learned*. In one workshop I've used the topic of crocodiles to teach some literacy strategies. First, we brainstorm what we know collectively about crocodiles, then we read a text and learn more while unlearning some of the misconceptions we may have had. With these strategies, all of which are pretty good and are based on how the brain learns, we are able to cover the curriculum.

But, imagine what would happen if after we collected our combined knowledge about crocodiles we then asked essential questions before or while we continued reading and studying. The lesson would change from learning facts about crocodiles to uncovering that which is worth understanding or pondering. It might look like this:

> Many reptiles, like the dinosaur and other animals and plants, have become extinct. What is it about the crocodile that has allowed it to survive and thrive for millions of years? Why do some species survive and others die out? What characteristics does humankind have that help it survive? What might signal the end or altering of humankind? Is humankind the ultimate survivor? How might we adapt to our changing environment?

Closing Comments

This chapter has taken a rather circuitous route from the mechanics of videotaping (covered very well in the National Board portfolio instructions) to a discussion on the art of questioning. The essential elements in these video-based portfolio entries are not what the video looks like or if we hear all students' responses. Those are important considerations. The essence of these entries, however, is what is happening in your classroom. How do you engage with students? How do you capture their minds and propel them forward? How do you prepare your students for the world they are entering, one that will be challenging and hold many unknown. These are the essential questions leading to quality verbal interaction and empowering education.

And Still Another Closing Comment

Poet Pablo Neruda asks the best questions. Here are some of my favorites from *The Book of Questions:*

For a biology class:

- Why do trees conceal the splendor of their roots?
- Why do leaves commit suicide when they feel yellow?

For art:

- If the color yellow runs out with what will we make bread?
- Is there anything in the world sadder than a train standing in the rain?

For law:

- Who hears the regrets of thieving automobiles?

For religious studies:

- How many churches are there in heaven?
- If I have died and don't know it of whom do I ask the time?

And for philosophy:

- Why don't they train helicopters to suck honey from the sunlight?
- Does smoke talk with the clouds?
- Is it true our desires must be watered with dew?

The Teacher's Guide to National Board Certification

Writing the Portfolio Entries

The National Board provides excellent commentary about writing the portfolio entry. Take the time to read the section, "Writing About Teaching," found in the getting started section of the portfolio instructions. This section has evolved over the past half-dozen years in response to the questions candidates ask most frequently. The instructions are continually improving. As with the chapter on videotaping, I'm not going to repeat what the NB has already done well. I will, however, highlight some items for your special consideration and share some examples taken from my experience working with hundreds of NB candidates.

The portfolio entries call for description, analysis (explanation), and reflection. Refer to the use of the SOAPS strategy presented in Chapter 11. It applies as well to writing your portfolio. The following chart is a graphical representation of each type of writing, with multiple ways of looking at the writing, which we'll discuss in detail in the following pages.

Description	What?	Say/Do
Analysis/Explanation	So what?	Mean
Reflection	Then what?	Matter

Description

Description is a retelling, an explanation of what you did (not to be confused with why you did it). Description answers the question "What happened?" It is a clear, logical, and complete picture that sets the context for the analysis and reflection. The audience for your writing is other classroom teachers (the assessors), but don't assume everything you do is common practice across the nation. When in doubt, explain. The first time you use an acronym, write it out completely. If you refer to a particular purchased curriculum, provide a one-sentence descriptor (i.e., S___ Math is a fourth-grade math curriculum adopted by and required by my school district). Include the features that best explain what follows in the description and analysis, without providing more detail, and taking up more space, than is necessary. The key here is to provide sufficient detail for the assessor, who did not see you deliver your lesson(s), to see the activity.

Remember the Say—Mean—Matter strategy introduced in Chapter 1? Description is akin to the say or do portion. The assessors need to know the literal or surface features of your lesson(s) in order to understand the reasons why you made the choices you made, and the results that followed as demonstrated in the student artifacts you include.

A strong description is a showing and telling of what happened. What did you do? What were the students doing while you did what you did? You don't have to avoid analysis within your description; there will be some overlap as you'll see when you read through the writing samples provided in the portfolio instructions. If you respond to the guiding questions as you write, and have others read your entries early enough for you to revise, you're more likely to provide the complete description assessors will need to see your practice.

Analysis

Although analysis and reflection have common elements, they are not the same. Each offers an explanation of what you did *means,* or the *so what?* of your teaching. The analysis of what happened is supported by the evidence you provide in the student artifacts you include and in bits of conversations with students or others that you report. For example, you might write: *Student A demonstrated understanding when she wrote . . .* followed by a quote from the essay. Or you might note: *Student B's parent called to say how homework battles have ceased because he now understands the assignments.* Although specific references and quotes are not always necessary, they present convincing proof for the conclusions you draw. Instead of saying the student understood the concept, show the assessors where in the student response they will find the proof of student understanding. Show, don't tell. Rather than writing, "My students achieved the instructional goals," say, "Student A demonstrated knowledge when she said(or wrote) . . . "—then quote the student.

Analysis explains why what you did and what your students did *matters*. Teaching is not about students having fun, or doing a long list of activities that don't, taken together, lead to understanding what is worth knowing. Although we want to engage our students and we want them to find learning enjoyable, having fun is not the goal. Teachers frequently have difficulty explaining their instructional goals and why these goals are important for these students at this time. If you haven't identified your instructional goals, how will you know when the students achieve them? How will they know?

Practice, Practice, Practice

It's valuable to take a lesson you already do and use it to write a mock portfolio entry. Do you understand, and can you explain, the context of your teaching environment? What do you need to know about your students and the challenges they represent in order to prepare and to deliver meaningful lessons that will add value to their lives? How do you apply this knowledge as you teach? How will this strategy, in this lesson, add to your students' understanding? Why are these lessons meaningful and important for students as they move beyond the classroom? These are enormously challenging questions. The strength and value of the NB process lies in the asking of these questions and in their answers. My teaching changed dramatically when I responded to the challenges presented in these questions. At least 25 percent of my lessons got tossed out. They didn't pass the test of meaningful and important, or they weren't appropriate for my students, or they didn't add value to their lives. I continue to ask these same questions in my work with teachers. In this way I can often contribute to the knowledge that we as teachers need, to become even better at what we do.

Reflection

Reflection differs from analysis in that it is introspective. It's about the *Then what?* of your teaching. You've done this or that; you've explained why it was important, meaningful, and appropriate for your students; you've analyzed the student outcomes—*Then what?* Reflection is about what you've learned from the process of teaching. Accomplished teachers learn by experience, by thinking about what they do and how their actions impact students. We learn and improve by analyzing and reflecting on what we do well, and by admitting what doesn't work. Accomplished teachers aren't about: I've been doing this same lesson for twenty years and the students still don't get it. If the students don't get it, we need to change what we're doing. The National Board doesn't expect that your teaching is perfect. Certification recognizes accomplished teaching, not perfection. Teaching is far too complex to allow for a single way of doing things.

A word of caution here. I've read entries in which the candidates went beyond honesty in evaluating and reflecting on their teaching. They were brutal. They picked out every flaw, everything that didn't go well, and they highlighted every student who didn't learn. If the lesson was that bad, if you didn't accomplish your instructional goals—don't use that lesson in your entry! While some falling short of 100 percent is acceptable, a failure is not. If the lesson was a complete bust, even though you did learn from it, don't select it for your portfolio.

Another caution. If the series of lessons was dynamite, and you can provide evidence in the student artifacts that this was the case, don't feel you have to find flaws. You can reflect on how this series came to work so well, the steps you've taken as a professional to continue to perfect your craft. I know that it's difficult for most teachers to say, "Darn, I'm good." I also suffer from insecurities, but sometimes you have done a masterful job and you should acknowledge it.

Probably the closest I've ever come to this kind of perfection is in conducting student-led conferences. I knew they were working because of the students' total engagement and the parents' involvement. I wanted to shout, "Yes, this is what great teaching and learning looks like!" but all I could do was stand off to the side and try to hide the tears. These are the teaching moments; when you write about them in your portfolio entries, the assessors will empathize with you and enjoy your success. Don't shy away from well-deserved accolades, even if you're the one giving them to yourself.

Writing to Learn

We write in order to record events, to provide information, and to tell stories. But one of the most powerful ways to use writing is to learn—a strategy we don't use often enough in teaching. Writing about your practice provides not only documentation, it also helps you discover what you do as a teacher as well as how and what you and your students learn. I write a lot and have since I was very young. Sometimes I'm surprised by what I've written, by the insights I've gained through reflecting on my experiences. Writing helps me to make sense of my life, to study my own history and then move forward.

Most teachers who come to the National Board process are enriched by it. They improve their practice by writing about it. Closely examining and writing about student work gives us a way of directly relating our teaching to student learning. It's not that we can't do this on our own, or in other contexts, we certainly can, and should. It's that we seldom take the time to analyze and reflect on our practices. More than anything else, participating in the National Board process is the instructional goal. Writing about your teaching is equivalent to learning about your teaching.

Cohort Groups Revisited

I want to reaffirm the importance of working within a small cohort group, a subject I've devoted an entire chapter to, but one that is worth reinforcing in the context of writing your portfolio entries. What you learn through writing about your practice is powerful, but the insights gained through sharing your entries with your cohort group are invaluable. In addition to receiving assistance with the mechanics, your group will help you to clarify and complete your entries. Remember, the immediate goal is to provide clear, convincing, and consistent evidence in each entry that you have accomplished the targeted standards. Your cohort group, using the reflective questions, and/or other strategies you find helpful, will assist as you improve on and complete your entries.

Show and Tell

I want to share with you a real-life experience I had working with a teacher-candidate named Barbara. Her experience is not atypical; it's one this book is designed to help you avoid.

Perhaps I can best capture the frustration of many teacher-candidates by paraphrasing an old Nat King Cole love song: "If a picture paints a thousand words then why can't I paint you? The words will never show, the you I've come to know." This is the kind of frustration I hear most often when I'm working with candidates who are struggling with their writing. It's also what I see when I am asked to observe teachers considered outstanding by their peers and administrators, who don't achieve certification on their first attempt. These candidates may have a very deep knowing about their students, but capturing what they know escapes them. Or they fail to record the things they take for granted. Barbara, an accomplished teacher who didn't achieve the first time, has a dynamic practice, but her portfolio entries were bland by comparison.

One afternoon when I was working at UCLA I received a phone call from a principal. Barbara, one of her teachers, had received notice that she did not achieve certification; in fact, her scores were quite low. Neither Barbara nor the principal understood what had happened. Their first inclination was to assume there were flaws in the NB process, but because I had done some coaching in the school district and am known locally as the NB guru, the principal asked if I would stop by and meet a very disappointed Barbara, which I did.

When I entered after lunch Barbara's fourth-grade urban classroom was bustling with engaged youngsters. They were doing a math lesson, but there was little direct instruction going on. Several students wrote narrative stories featuring wheels and various configurations of passengers in a wide range of realistic and creative vehicles. Another group, seated around a table covered with manipulatives, were having a heated exchange. Still another group worked with the teacher asking her and one another as many questions as they were answering. Off in a corner the classroom featured a miniature hothouse overflowing with greenery. Hamsters ran through a habitat in another corner of the room. Movement was everywhere. During the afternoon youngsters shared their math stories and portfolio collections with me. I frequently do classroom observations and I tend to be fairly critical, usually seeing past the surface features of a classroom in order to uncover the underlying structure. Barbara's practice exhibited all the features I'd look for if I were looking to place one of my own children in a new class. Still, her NB scores were low.

At the end of the day, after the students had left, Barbara and I talked about her practice. She was articulate, tuned into the youngsters I asked about, and had sound reasons for the strategies I'd observed during the day. Then we looked at a copy of the portfolio entries she had submitted to the National Board. At that time there were six required entries compared to the four the Board now requires. Yet, even with six entries her portfolio was thin. Entries that allowed for twelve pages had fewer than half that number.

Red Flag!

Pay attention to the page allocations provided in the instructions. These are not arbitrary numbers. Each portfolio entry is field-tested. Based on the pilot entries, the Board carefully analyzes, among other things, the

The Teacher's Guide to National Board Certification

total number of pages necessary for a strong response. These are the maximum number of pages per entry and also the recommended number of pages for particular parts of an entry. Pay heed. If your final response falls way short, like Barbara's did, you are probably not fully responding to the guiding questions nor providing clear, consistent, and convincing evidence of all the targeted standards. The general rule I use with my candidates is the 15 percent page measure. If you're short of the maximum space allowed by much more than that, you may want to rethink the entry. Barbara had huge gaps in her responses for each entry.

Second Red Flag Alert!

Another distinguishing feature of Barbara's portfolio was its extreme modesty. Barbara had failed to toot her own horn. I know that is very difficult for many candidates; it is something we often talk about in our groups. In general, teachers are modest, especially the great ones. We don't have forums for praising ourselves or the work we do. We're more likely to focus on the child who didn't improve and who still has some problems we haven't been able to solve, rather than boast about the many youngsters whose lives we've added value to each year. When I asked Barbara why she hadn't written about some of the extraordinary ways her students were demonstrating their own accomplishments, she shrugged me off. Because those are ordinary, she seemed to say. I'd been in enough classrooms to know they were not, that Barbara was indeed accomplished.

Boast. Every teacher is not doing all the wonderful things you are with your students. Not every teacher has the deep understanding of what each student needs and how to help that student to achieve. The portfolio is not the place to be modest. When I attended the scoring institute several years ago, one of the National Board folks estimated in an aside that fewer than 20 percent of teachers then in the classroom would fall in the 3 or 4 category as measured by the NB standards. I hope that figure is rising. If your students are doing well, give yourself the credit you deserve.

In addition to their brevity and very modest stance, Barbara's entries had huge gaps. She assumed the assessors would fill in the blanks. Her descriptions of the lessons and activities lacked detail. The snapshot she'd provided didn't provide a clear picture for the assessors to see her classroom practice. Although the assessors are all teachers of your grade and subject, teaching—even great teaching—has so many variables we need to spell them out. On the other hand, our audience is educators, not the general public, so there are some assumptions you can make. The balance between enough detail and too much is difficult to ascertain. The question becomes: What is important to include in the description so the assessor can understand the context of this lesson or to understand the analysis of this student's work?

A Word to the Wise

Do have others read your entries. Listen when they ask you to fill in the missing gaps. Use the reflective conversation questions to draw out the necessary information.

The Happy Ending

Barbara didn't have to revamp her teaching practice in order to achieve certification, she just had to write about it more fully. The following year, after Barbara received her scores, notably high, she sent me a note and gift certificate. Although I enjoyed spending the certificate in one of our local department stores, I have kept the note. She wrote: *Thank you for giving me back my self-esteem.* I can't take credit for having done that. Barbara's accomplished teaching was already in place; her students' achievements were proof of that. I just asked the questions that helped Barbara to capture her teaching in writing. She did the rest.

References

Adelman, H., and L. Taylor. 2002. *New Directions for School and Community Initiatives to Address Barriers to Learning: Two Examples of Concept Papers to Inform and Guide Policy Makers* (Concept paper). Los Angeles: University of California, Los Angeles.

Archer, J. 1997. *Bad News About Bad Teaching,* Retrieved from website: *www.edweek.org/ew/vol-16/19ideas.h16.*

Archer, J. 1999, (May 5). *Sanders 101.* Retrieved from website.

Bell, J. A. 2001. *High-performing, High-poverty Schools.* Sacramento: Statewide System of School Support (S4).

Bond, L., Ph.D. 2000. "Accomplished Teaching Validation Study" (Research study). Arlington: University of North Carolina, Greensboro.

Bransford, J. D., A. L. Brown, and R. R. Cocking, (Eds.). 2000. *How People Learn.* Washington, D.C.: National Academy Press.

Carr, J. F., and D. E. Harris. 2001. *Succeeding With Standards: Linking Curriculum, Assessment, and Action Planning.* Alexandria: Association for Supervision and Curriculum Development.

Cohen, R. M. 2002. "Schools Our Teachers Deserve: A Proposal for Teacher-centered Reform." *Phi Delta Kappan 83 (March):* 532–533.

Costa, A. L., and R. J. Garmston, 1994. *Cognitive Coaching: A Foundation for Renaissance Schools.* Norwood: Christopher-Gordon Publishers, Inc.

Csikszentmihalyi, M. 1997. *Finding Flow: The Psychology of Engagement with Everyday Life* (1st ed.). New York: HarperCollins Basic Books.

Darling-Hammond, L. 1999. *"Educating Teachers for California's Future."* Paper presented at the Teacher Education Summit of California College and University Presidents, Stanford University. (December 6).

Elmore, R. F. (2000). *Building a New Structure for School Leadership* (Report). Washington DC: The Albert Shanker Institute.

Falk, B. 2000. *The Heart of the Matter.* Portsmouth, NH: Heinemann.

Finn, P. J. 1999. *Literacy With an Attitude* (1st ed.). Albany: State University of New York Press.

Gardner, H. 1999. *The Disciplined Mind: What All Students Should Understand.* New York City: Simon & Schuster.

Glasser, W., M.D. 1993. *The Quality School Teacher: A Companion Volume to the Quality School.* New York: HarperPerennial, a division of HarperCollins, *Publishers.*

Graves, D. H. 2001. *The Energy to Teach.* Portsmouth: Heinemann.

Goldman, Daniel. 1995. *Emotional Intelligence: Why It Can Matter More Than IQ.* Bantam Book: New York City.

Hawley, W. D. (Ed.). 2002. *The Keys to Effective Schools*. Thousand Oaks: Corwin Press, Inc.

Haycock, K. 1998. *Good Teaching Matters: How Well-qualified Teachers Can Close the Gap* (Report, Vol. 3, Issue 2). Washington, D.C.: Education Trust, Inc.

Haycock, K. 2000. "Exceeding expectations." *Restructuring Brief 23:* 1–8.

Johnson, S., M.D. 1998. *Who Moved My Cheese?* New York: Putnam.

Keene, E. O., and S. Zimmermann. 1997. *Mosaic of Thought*. Portsmouth: Heinemann.

Neruda, Pablo. *The Book of Questions.* 1974. Translated by William O'Daly. Copper Canyon Press: Port Townsend. (Posthumous publication). ISBN 1-55659-040-7. Original title: *El Libro de las preguntas.*

Noguera, P. A. 2002. "Beyond Size: The Challenge of High School Reform. *Educational Leadership 59* (February 2002): 60–63.

Reeves, D. B., Ph.D. 1998. *Making Standards Work* (2nd ed.). Denver: Center for Performance Assessment.

Routman, R. 2002. "Teacher Talk." *Educational Leadership 59* (March): 32–35.

Sanders, W., and J. Rivers. 1996. "*Cumulative and Residual Effects of Teachers on Future Student Academic Achievement* (Research progress report). Knoxville: University of Tennessee Value-Added Research and Assessment Center.

Scheurich, J. J., and L. Skrla. 2001. "Continuing the Conversation on Equity and Accountability: Listening Appreciatively, Responding Responsibly." *Phi Delta Kappan:* 322–326.

Schmoker, M. 1996. *Results* (1st ed.). Alexandria: Association for Supervision and Curriculum Development.

Stigler, J. W., and J. Hiebert. 2001. *The Teaching Gap: Best Ideas from the World's Teachers for Improving Education in the Classroom*. New York: The Free Press.

The Education Trust, I. 2001. "*Achievement in America, 2000.*" Paper presented at the Association of California School Administrators, Los Angeles, California. (April 3).

Thornburg, D. 2002. *The New Basics: Education and the Future of Work in the Telematic Age* (1st ed.). Alexandria: Association for Supervision and Curriculum Development.

Tyack, D. B. 1974. *The One Best System: A History of American Urban Education* (1st ed.). Cambridge: Harvard University Press.

Vygotsky, Lev. *How People Learn: Brain, Mind, Experience, and School.* Editors: M. Suzanne Donovan, John D. Bransford, and James W. Pellegrino. National Research Council. National Academy Press. Washington, D.C.

Wiggins, G., and J. McTighe. 1998. *Understanding by Design*. Alexandria: Association for Supervision and Curriculum Development.

Willis, S. 2002. "Creating a Knowledge Base for Teaching: A Conversation with James Stigler." *Educational Leadership, 59 (March):* 6–11.

Wolfe, P. 2001. *Brain Matters: Translating Research into Classroom Practice.* Alexandria: Association for Supervision and Curriculum Development.

Author's email address: *nbpts@sbcglobal.net*

Author's Website: *www.accomplishedteaching.com*

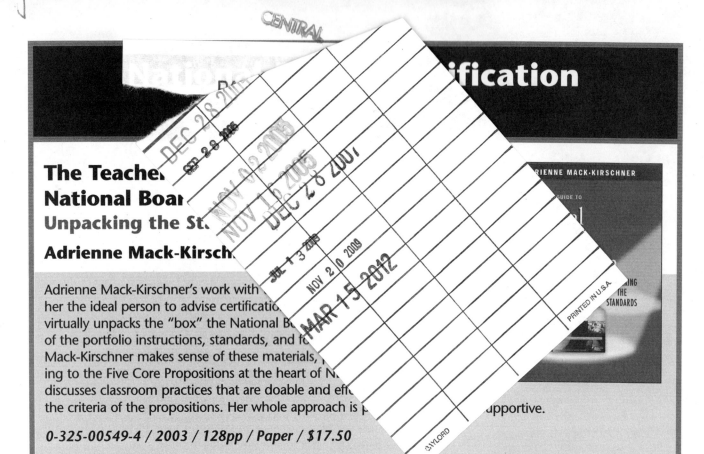